The Structure of the World Economy and Prospects for a New International Economic Order

PERGAMON
POLICY
STUDIES

ON THE NEW INTERNATIONAL
ECONOMIC ORDER

UNITAR/CEESTEM Library on NIEO

The Structure of the World Economy and Prospects for a New International Economic Order

Edited by
Ervin Laszlo
Joel Kurtzman

A volume in the New International
Economic Order (NIEO) Library
Published for UNITAR and the
Center for Economic and Social
Studies of the Third World (CEESTEM)

Pergamon Press
NEW YORK • OXFORD • TORONTO • SYDNEY • FRANKFURT • PARIS

Pergamon Press Offices:

U.S.A   Pergamon Press Inc., Maxwell House, Fairview Park,
                       Elmsford, New York 10523, U.S.A.

U.K.   Pergamon Press Ltd., Headington Hill Hall,
                       Oxford OX3 0BW, England

CANADA   Pergamon of Canada Ltd., 150 Consumers Road,
                       Willowdale, Ontario M2J 1P9, Canada

AUSTRALIA   Pergamon Press (Aust) Pty. Ltd., P.O. Box 544,
                       Potts Point, NSW 2011, Australia

FRANCE   Pergamon Press SARL, 24 rue des Ecoles,
                       75240 Paris, Cedex 05, France

FEDERAL REPUBLIC   Pergamon Press GmbH, 6242 Kronberg/Taunus,
OF GERMANY   Pferdstrasse 1, Federal Republic of Germany

Library of Congress Cataloging in Publication Data

Main entry under title:

The Structure of the world economy and prospects for a
new international economic order.

(Pergamon policy studies on the new international
economic order)
    Includes bibliographies and index.
    1. International economic relations—Addresses,
essays, lectures. I. Laszlo, Ervin, 1932-
II. Kurtzman, Joel, III. Series.
HF1411.S844 1980   382.1   79-23350
ISBN 0-08-025119-6

Printed in the United States of America

Contents

Preface to the UNITAR-CEESTEM NIEO Library

Ervin Laszlo

The present volume is one in a series of 17 books which make up the UNITAR-CEESTEM NIEO Library. While each volume covers a specific aspect of the issues that comprise the New International Economic Order and can be read independently of the others, it seems useful to provide a brief introduction to outline the scope of the entire undertaking and put this volume in its proper context.

In the winter of 1976-77 UNITAR (the United Nations Institute for Training and Research) initiated with CEESTEM (the Centro de Estudios Economicos y Sociales del Tercer Mundo, Mexico) a series of inquiries into problems and opportunities associated with the establishment of the New International Economic Order (NIEO). Both institutions agreed that the NIEO constituted one of the highest priority items on the international agenda, and that independent, objective, and scholarly investigation of its objectives, obstacles, opportunities, and indicated strategies may be of great value both to the decision makers directly concerned with the negotiation of the issues, and to the international community at large. The UNITAR-CEESTEM NIEO Library is a result of the research that was undertaken by the central professional staffs of the institutes, and by their jointly formed international network of collaborators and consultants.

What are some of the reasons behind this assessment of the importance of the NIEO in contemporary economic and world affairs? Although most people know that the world economy is encountering serious difficulties on both national and international levels, few people outside a small circle of experts realize the seriousness of the problems and the breadth of their scope. Contrary to some current perceptions, the NIEO is neither a passing pressure of the poor countries on the rich, nor merely a demand for more aid and assistance. It is a process which has deep historical precedents, and an undisputed historical significance.

We need not go back further than the end of World War II to find an entire array of historical events which set the stage for the later emergence of the call for the NIEO. While these events arose from their own historical antecedents, they themselves produced the setting for the breakdown of the post-war economic system, and the widening gap between rich and poor nations.

The first and perhaps most decisive event was the liberation of the oppressed peoples of Africa and Asia, in the great wave of decolonization that swept the world in the year following World War II. The newly independent states were said to be sovereign and equal to all other states, old and new, large and small. Their admittance to the U.N. underscored this. However, the fresh political and juridical status of the new countries was far from matched by their actual economic conditions. The majority felt that their de jure political colonization ended only to be replaced by a de facto economic colonization.

The historical process which gave the majority of the world's population the status of citizens of sovereign and equal states, but left them at the same time in a situation of economic underdevelopment and dependence, triggered the "revolution of rising expectations". Desires for rapid economic growth led Third World governments into ambitious plans and programmes of national development. Most of the plans envisaged a quick repetition of the industrial growth processes of the developed world, following a path already long trodden by the countries of Latin America. When the unintended side-effects of traditional patterns of industrialization became evident – uncontrolled growth of cities, relative neglect of rural areas and agriculture, threats to the environment, and the increasing stratification of people in modern and traditional sectors, often with serious damage to social structure and cohesion – many of the original development strategies underwent modification. However, the goal of rapid economic growth was not surrendered. Quantitative growth targets were formally included in the official development strategies of the First and Second U.N. Development Decades (for the 1960s and the 1970s, respectively).

However, the mid-term review of the achievement of the Second Development Decade's goals showed mixed results. The greatest disappointment came in the area of agricultural production and official development aid. On the average, the U.N. official development aid targets have not even been half achieved. At the same time, service charges on past loans began to put enormous pressures on developing countries' balance of payment, and world poverty showed no signs of diminishing. There was insufficient progress in commodity trade, inadequate access to the markets of developed countries, particularly for agricultural products; tariffs have escalated, especially for semi-processed and processed products, and new tariff and nontariff restrictions were introduced by many developed countries on a number of items, including textiles and leather goods. The plight of the least developed, island and land-locked developing countries, gave rise to additional concern. While some progress was achieved, for example, through the introduction of a generalized system of preferences by the developed countries, and the proposals of the Tokyo Declaration concerning multilateral trade negotiations, the negative developments weighed more heavily in the balance and created widespread dissatisfaction in the developing world.

Another set of factors came into play as well. This was the sudden and unexpected rise of Third World economic and political power. The Middle East oil embargo of 1972-1973, and the subsequent four-fold increase in the price of oil created a world energy crisis. It affected all oil importing nations, developed as well as developing. It also exhibited the dependence of the developed countries on the developing world for several major natural resources, and proved the ability of the Third World to wield economic and political power effectively. The consequences included rises in the price of food, due to the increased cost of chemical fertilizers, and further tensions between producers and consumers of raw materials. But the OPEC-type exercise of Third World economic and political power proved unable to improve the condition of the developing countries as a whole. Despite significantly higher gross resource flows from the oil-exporting to the oil-importing developing countries, the economic plight of the latter worsened due to the higher cost of energy. Developed countries found themselves beset by economic problems of their own, including not only higher oil prices but inflation, unemployment, and unused industrial capacity. Economic rates of growth slowed, while in most countries balance of payment deficits grew. Even where surpluses could still be generated, concerns focused on the domestic economy, and political will to increase levels of aid and assistance to the Third World faltered.

Compounding the economic difficulties of the developed nations were signs of breakdown in the international monetary system which affected all countries, developed as well as developing. Amidst growing tensions between the United States, Japan and the European Community over matters of trade, the Bretton Woods system collapsed and gave rise to a system of floating exchange rates. The value of the U.S. dollar began to erode, creating serious difficulties for those countries which, like most of the Third World, held their reserves in dollars. The creation of Special Drawing Rights provided some access to foreign exchange independently of dollar holdings, but such access favored the countries already developed, and the rest remained seriously dissatisfied with the workings of the international monetary system. It became evident that some of the fundamental tenets of the post-war world economy were being called into question, and indeed that some had already collapsed.

The NIEO made its appearance as an international political issue in the context of this series of events. Encouraged by the success of OPEC but fearful of splintering Third World solidarity through the newly won wealth of a few of its countries, Presidents Boumedienne of Algeria and Echeverria of Mexico, among others, called for structural reforms in the international economic system. Their governments' initiative resulted in the adoption of such major U.N. resolutions as those of the Sixth and Seventh Special Session, and the Charter of Economic Rights and Duties of States. These in turn provided the impetus for a long series of declarations, resolutions, position papers and studies on various NIEO issues by the United Nations system and the international community at large.

The coming together of these historical factors was not purely coincidental. The wave of decolonization was the culmination of a long-term historical process of democratization, and the rise of the concept of universal rights for individuals and societies. It led, in turn, to a mounting desire for rapid industrialization by the newly independent countries. This met with major frustrations. But as economic inter-dependence intensified, as trade and markets expanded, and access to energy and raw materials became crucial to the developed world's giant economic machinery, the concentration of economic power itself was modified. It was no longer wielded by a few powerful governments but also fell into the hands of oil exporting nations and transnational corporations.

The historical process which gave birth to a host of independent nation-states placed into sharp relief the inequities of the previous economic system, and provided some of the developing countries with fresh degrees of economic leverage. Since they not only control the supply of a number of important fuels and raw materials but also absorb about 25 percent of the developed world's exports, their demands can no longer be ignored. And they insist that a healthy growth in the world economy cannot be brought about within the framework of the existing economic system.

When the General Assembly, in December, 1977 called for another Special Session in 1980 to assess progress in the establishment of the NIEO, it took a decisive step in bringing the North-South debate to the Organization, where it belongs. It created an ongoing forum for discussions and negotiation in the interim through the Committee of the Whole, which during 1978 managed to define its role and function despite earlier disagreements. Together with the work of the bodies charged with the preparation of the International Development Strategy for the Third United Nations Development Decade, the Organization created the fora for substantive progress in the area of restructuring the economic relations of developed and developing countries. Faced with mounting pressures on national economics in all parts of the world, the international community now finds itself facing a watershed deci-sion: to make use of these fora, or to continue to use mainly bilateral and sectoral corrective measures to mitigate tensions while entrusting the resolution of problems to the mechanisms of the free market.

This decision is intimately linked to an entire array of basic questions. Among them:

The question of cost and benefit. Who will have to bear the burden of instituting NIEO and will the results be worth the sacrifices? Will benefits really accrue to the poor people to help fulfill their basic needs and will developing countries be made truly more self-reliant – or will the main beneficiaries be the already rich elites? Will the developed countries also benefit from NIEO (a positive-sum game) or will it mainly mean the redistribution of the current stock of wealth from them to the developing countries (a zero-sum game)?

The question of legitimacy. Is the free market the basic mechanism of world trade and the best vehicle of development, or is it merely a convenient fiction to cover up the current unjust manipulations of the major economic groups?

The question of morality. Do the rich countries have a moral obligation to help the poor, and especially the poorest? Does this responsibility extend to those countries who had no historical part in the creation of poverty in the third world?

The question of political feasibility. How strongly will different organized groups in society support or oppose governmental policies aimed at the achievement of the NIEO – and how much solidarity exists in these domains internationally, among the developing and the developed countries themselves?

It is unrealistic to expect that real progress will be made on specific NIEO issues (such as official development aid, technical assistance, debt renegotiation, removal of tariff barriers, technical co-operation among developing countries, the link between SDRs and development, voting power in the World Bank and IMF, transfers of technology, regulation of transnational corporations, a system of consultations on industrialization, and restructuring the economic and social sectors of the United Nations) so long as the basic issues are not resolved and a consensus does not emerge concerning them. NIEO can be achieved if, and only if, it is perceived that its benefits are universal and can reach all segments of the world's population (especially the neediest); if it is held that its costs do not exceed its benefits; if its regulatory mechanisms are seen to be legitimate; if some real sense of moral responsibility exists among members of the human community, and if sufficient political support is available nationally as well as internationally for the indicated measures. If one or more of these preconditions are not met, the NIEO will not be achieved; Member States will continue to practice the existing, predominantly piecemeal, ad hoc and mainly bilateral modes of adjusting to stresses and reaching compromises.

The basic pupose of the UNITAR-CEESTEM NIEO Library is to provide an independent and objective assessment of these issues, and to report its findings in time for the historic events of 1980: the Special Session of the General Assembly devoted to the assessment of progress toward the NIEO, and the immediatley following regular session, during which the International Development Strategy for the 1980s and beyond (the U.N.'s Third Development Decade) is to be debated and adopted. It would be clearly an enormous waste of time and effort to enter into these negotiations without forming a clear idea of the issues that bear on their success. But reporting on them is not a simple matter of using insight and intuition; it requires painstaking and organized empirical research. The requirement is to identify the forces that operate for or against the NIEO in all parts of the world. Intuitive answers concerning its cost and benefits, legitimacy, morality, and political feasibility occur to all persons knowledgeable in these areas, but such answers tend to vary and are thus not sufficiently reliable. Expert research on the current obstacles and opportunities associated with the NIEO in the different regions of the world, and with respect to the diverse sectors of the world economy, needs to be conducted. The results of such research may shed some much needed light on the chances of success in establishing a new international economic order generally, and on the types of objectives and modes of negotiations that, in the positive case, could lead to it specifically. For although it is unlikely that a dominant consensus already exists in the world concerning the cost and benefit, legitimacy, morality, and political feasibility of the NIEO (if it did exist, the international community would probably not be experiencing the sense of frustration it has today), the precise estimation of costs versus benefits, legitimacy versus illegitimacy, morality versus indifference, and political feasibility versus futility by different societal groups could reveal highly differentiated potentials for achieving a dominant consensus in the future. Today's chaotic welter of opinions and pressures concerning the NIEO need not remain such, but could crystallize into a decisive mood favoring or opposing it. To those who object to such analysis on the grounds that economic theory, rather than wide-ranging socio-political considerations, must serve to decide the fate of NIEO, we may reply that economic theory, while relevant, is in itself over generous: it can often prove both sides of conflicting positions. Since both sides in a dispute can marshal some variety of economic theory in their defence, and no common criteria exist for assessing the relative merits of all theories, economic rationality as conveyed by economic theories becomes marginal in the negotiating process. We need to go one step deeper, inquiring into the reasons particular theories are summoned to defend particular points of view, as well as measuring the intensity of commitment to these viewpoints and the negotiating power of the parties subscribing to them.

Thus, the focus of the UNITAR-CEESTEM Library is not a given economic theory, but the perceptions and opinions underlying the positions taken by diverse actors. The configuration and strength of these perceptions and opinions will ultimately determine whether negotiations in the area of the NIEO can be successful, and if so, which strategies will have optimum chances of success.

The Library contains volumes arranged in three different series. First, there is a series of overview studies. These provide background, context, and basic reference data. They include a volume defining and classifying the principal objectives of the NIEO as agreed or debated in the United Nations and other major international fora; a volume giving an overview and assessment of alternative viewpoints on the NIEO espoused by various nongovernmental groups and researchers and different parts of the world; a third defining the most critical obstacles confronting the establishment of the NIEO; a fourth dealing with the specific problems of food and agriculture as they are debated in the framework of the United Nations. A fifth volume suggests the basic strategies which appear indicated and appropriate to accelerate progress toward the NIEO; and a final volume communicates the results of the associated UNITAR-CEESTEM International Opinion Survey of Decision-Makers and Experts on the crucial questions of the NIEO.

The second series contains geographic studies. Volumes in this series review the positions and postures of national governments and the attitudes of business, labor, the public media, and the opinion of the population at large in various nations and regions of the world. Individual volumes focus on the United States and Canada, on Western Europe, on Eastern Europe including the Soviet Union, on Asia including Australia, on Latin America, and on Africa and the Middle East.

The third series of the NIEO Library is devoted to functional studies. Here experts give their views and assessments of such issues as the possible and the desirable structure of the world economy; of the patterns and problems of international trade and industrial development; of international financial matters, and of the associated political and institutional, as well as social and cultural problems and opportunities.

Among them, the seventeen volumes of the Library cover practically all the principal issues encountered in efforts to establish a New International Economic Order, through in-depth discussion by independent investigators, coming from different societies in different parts of the world.

The UNITAR-CEESTEM NIEO Library offers wide-ranging analyses, and sometimes divergent viewpoints, on a broad range of topics. It does not offer simplistic solutions, nor advocate one viewpoint indiscriminately over others. It seeks to illuminate the range and complexity of the issues, provide clarification of individual items, and to lend a sense of the vastness and significance of the NIEO as a whole.

It is the hope of all of us, researchers and consultants of the UNITAR-CEESTEM project on the NIEO, that our results, published as the NIEO Library, may render some service to the decisionmaker and negotiator who must cope with the problems of the international economic order, as well as to the student of international economic and world affairs, interested in further research on these topics. It is our view that the NIEO is a historically necessary, and humanly and politically appropriate attempt to create a world order that is sustainable for generations, equitable for all, and capable of meeting the most urgent needs and demands of the peoples and nations of the world community.

Ervin Laszlo

Project Director

Introduction
Ervin Laszlo
Joel Kurtzman

Demands and proposals for a new international economic order and the actual establishment of such an order are two different things. Proposals can be made in the framework of conferences and assemblies within and outside the United Nations, and they may be incorporated in resolutions agreed upon in principle by the entire international community. Such acts have real value in promoting knowledge and understanding of the NIEO, and signaling dominant perceptions and policy postures on the part of member states. However, these acts do not normally have a legally binding and internationally enforceable character. The step from proposals and demands to resolutions and principles is a major one; it has been taken in a number of significant instances in the past few years. However, the step from resolutions to actual implementation is a giant one and, with exceptions, it has not been taken yet. This is a cause for dissatisfaction on the part of proponents of the NIEO, and constitutes the reason why the international economic order of the 1950s and the 1960s is still with us in the 1970s. If something better and more equitable is to develop by the 1980s, principles will have to be translated into concrete measures.

Action in the real world never takes place in a vacuum. It enters a stream of relations, conditions, and perceptions, which it modifies and by which it is modified in turn. New policies must be effectively superimposed on old ones; loyalties must actively switch from entrenched categories of values to new ideals and goals. In a word, innovative action must alter the <u>structure</u> of existing values and relationships. In the context of this volume, policies aimed at achieving a new and more equitable international economic order must alter the existing structure of the world economy.

This, then, is the crux of the matter concerning the NIEO. It must impact on a complex and still solidly entrenched international economic structure, overcome forces and relations that were evolved to maintain and protect this structure, and create new forces aimed at the maintenance and protection of a new structure.

A number of requirements flow immediately from this observation. First, the specifics of the existing structure of the world economy must be adequately understood. This implies a knowledge of the historical processes which called it into being and of the social, political, psychological, and cultural forces which have come to stabilize it. Second, an analysis of the relationship between the existing structure of the world economy and the general principles of a NIEO is called for. It is as important to know what needs to be changed as it is to know what needs to be achieved. Means and ends have to be related; the objectives of the NIEO have to be brought into functional relationship with the structure and the forces of the present world economy. Third, the political will and wisdom to act on the foregoing insights needs to be marshalled. And fourth, there must be solidarity, persistence, and goodwill in the long and difficult negotiations which appear to be the sine qua non of moving beyond declarations and resolutions to the realm of concerted international action.

This volume, like intellectual research in general, can do little to contribute directly to the third and fourth requirements of the establishment of the NIEO, unless by generating support for moral convictions and courage for taking calculated risks in policy innovation. But it can offer a modest yet not insignificant contribution to the first and second areas. In Part One, it illuminates some of the key features of the current world economic structure. And in Part Two, it relates the principles of the NIEO to the existing world situation in economic, political, as well as the crucial yet often neglected juridical areas.

It would be misleading, however, to oversimplify the complexity of the task involved in these attempts, or to underestimate its magnitude. It is only in the most evolved natural sciences that general agreement tends to persist for any length of time on the description of the nature of the phenomena in question. If there is a level of agreement on the structure of the atom, or the structure of the astronomical universe (and underlying such agreement there is often a large number of minute disagreements and competing concepts and theories), it is because neither atoms nor galaxies have a conscious will, nor do they hold opinions about themselves and their surroundings which may be divorced from the real state of affairs in the universe. Human beings do, however, possess conscious volition, and they do hold views and embrace values and attitudes which may or may not coincide with the real nature of the world in which they live. Moreover this world is to a large extent their own collective creation (which does not exclude the individually false views concerning many of its aspects), and their perceptions impact on their surroundings and alter its structures and processes. It is little wonder, then, that social scientists, even in such relatively highly evolved fields as economics, should hold conflicting views. It is even less surprising that policy makers, acquainted in practice with only a part of the complex web of interrelationships that makes up the world economy, should make shaky assumptions about the structure of international economic relations and the effects of policies upon them.

In view of the multiple uncertainties of analysis, it would be foolhardy to speak of an objective and definitive description of the structure of the contemporary world economy. At best, we can provide various perspectives, each treating the world economic structure through the filter of a particular body of concepts, values, assumptions and theories. In order to reduce the number of possible perceptions to manageable dimensions, and to ensure relevance to the paramount task of examining the forms of implementation of a new international economic order, the perspectives must be restricted to those which affect the structure of the world economy. That is, the perspectives must be representative of the dominant policy making forces in the contemporary world. What results may not be a depiction of economic and social reality in its pristine objectivity, but it will constitute an assessment of that reality in the light of forces and factors that shape it.

Part One contains analyses of the structure of the world economy from three distinct perspectives. These correspond to – though they may not consciously represent – the dominant varieties of societal forces guiding the destiny of the world economy: the Northern perspective of the free market industrial economies, the Southern perspective of the developing countries, and the socialist perspective of the leftist countries. The debate on the NIEO is thus enriched by an examination of the structures and relations which the NIEO would alter or replace, as seen from the standpoint of the major actors in the debate.

It is not the intention of the editors to suggest, however, that the studies included in Part One are one-dimensional or biased. Each is consistent within its own framework of concepts and values, and the reader will quite properly agree with those that share his or her own concepts and values. We merely suggest that all perspectives should command attention, for all represent internally consistent descriptions and throw light on the forces that mold the economic and social future of the world.

The analyses contained in Part One speak for themselves, and only brief remarks are needed to highlight their key conclusions. The Northern perspective, illustrated here in the work of Michael Hudson, is not that of classical economics (itself a Northern, more specifically a Western viewpoint), but one of economic rationality in a historical framework. Industrialization policies and the constant optimization of productivity factors are seen as the crucial achievements of the Northern free market economies. Although these countries had the fewest advantages in terms of natural resources, their high level of technological sophistication, skilled and well-paid labor force, evolved urban and social infrastructure, and abundant liquid investment capital enabled them to become the main pillars of the contemporary world economy. Currently their well-paid labor can undersell the low-wage labor of developing countries when costs are adjusted on a unit basis. The problems of the Third World are seen to reside mainly in its low and still deteriorating factoral (productivity-adjusted) terms of trade, which make its economies uncompetitive on world markets and create conditions of dependence. By selling their nonrenewable mineral resources to pay for renewable agricultural products and finished industrial goods, they force themselves into debt and economic obsolescence. More investment is needed in domestic Third World infrastructures, and in the social conditions which raise skill levels and productivity functions. Developing countries should have access to international capital for such investment, and there must be a corresponding revision of the austerity condition currently attached to borrowing from international financial institutions. The study affirms – unlike some other Northern views – that the problems of the world economy have now become structural. The above-mentioned factors threaten a split into two polarized factions – the high-productivity Northern, and the low-productivity Southern economies. In the long term this would not serve the interest of either side.

In the first of two studies conveying a Southern perspective on the structure of the world economy, Aldo Ferrer traces today's economic difficulties to the diminishing hegemony of the United States economy and the emergence of the European community and Japan as major economic actors. The "center" of the world economy came to embrace the trilateral countries, reinforced by strong internal markets. Expansion occurred within the framework of this market, at the expense of the periphery. Raw materials and foodstuffs declined in importance in the overall expenditures of the countries of the center, while synthetics and related factors made for a slow growth in the world demand for primary products. All this contributed to the rapid decline of the participation of the periphery countries in world trade. The declining value of the dollar, the creation of the Euro-markets, and the increased liquidity of the private sector created an unordered form of international economic expansion in which the developing countries could not properly participate. They remained trapped in the vicious circle of specialized export of primary goods and growing demand for manufactures. The developed countries give only passing attention to these problems of the Third World: official development aid, the generalized system of preferences, and similar measures function mainly as temporary palliatives. Currently, the trilateral system is faced with an internal crisis as well as mounting challenges from the Third World. Global interdependencies, political instabilities, and rapidly depleting natural resources give new importance today to the countries of the Third World. While they are more and more tied to the countries of the world economic center, in the perspective represented here the developing countries themselves must make the critical decisions if their marginal role in the world economy is to be overcome.

Another Southern perspective, developed by Enrique Oteiza and his collaborators, uses a basically Marxist conceptual framework to analyze the structure of the contemporary world economy and to explain why change in the real world does not conform to the shape of a new order demanded by the developing countries. Forces exercising hegemony in the countries of the center attempt to preserve the present distribution of wealth and power, acting in a transnational framework. But the world economy is in deep crisis. As the capitalist countries concentrate on resolving the symptoms of the crisis they created — inflation, unemployment, financial problems — the developing countries bear the weight of the transfer of the crisis to their own economies in the form of deteriorating terms of trade, reduction of export markets, increasing costs of debt servicing, and so on. The implantation of hegemony-wielding groups within these countries adds to the effects of the crisis in the Third World, and reinforces the patterns of dependence. Recent negotiations have shown that the developed countries are not willing to compromise their positions in favor of the Third World; they do not wish to abandon the status quo in regard to interference in the free market system, or their control over economic processes that affect developing countries. The reason for this is seen to lie in the requirements of the contemporary form of capitalism, which needs constant expansion of markets, raw materials, and capital. What integration occurs on the world level is promoted by transnational corporations and may represent more of a further evolution of the current economic system than a change toward a new and just economic order.

There are broad divergences in the perceptions of the structure of the world economy in these perspectives. There are also, however, some fundamental agreements. All studies agree that the difficulties experienced today in all economies are not of a temporary and accidental, but of a long-term and structural character. All agree that basic structural reforms are needed to correct current imbalances and inequities. And all favor some variety of a new international economic order, while stressing different aspects and assigning divergent priorities to its objectives.

The three studies that constitute Part Two of the present volume do not attempt to relate the principles of the NIEO to the structure of the world economy as conveyed by the foregoing analyses — a task well beyond the limits and ambitions of this book — but present independent studies of a number of crucial aspects related to structural considerations in the contemporary economic system.

Miguel Wionczek diagnoses past failures in NIEO negotiations and assesses future prospects. He defines the areas in which negotiations are presently deadlocked, points out that some of the current NIEO objectives would stabilize the existing economic system rather than contribute to its restructuring, and allocates responsibility for past failures to all sides in the debate. He suggests the inclusion of additional actors in the negotiations (especially transnational corporations and members of the growing international public system). The relations of TNCs to the NIEO considerably exceed the single item of a code of conduct for their operations. Little progress toward a new order can be expected until these corporations are adequately involved in all phases of the negotiations, and developing countries achieve a modus vivendi with respect to them. Likewise, the United Nations and other members of the emerging global public system must become involved and organized. Prospects for the establishment of the NIEO depend critically, however, on the perceptions and policies of the developing countries themselves. North-South economic issues are but one element in a complex set of issues which must be resolved if real progress is to be made: between East and West, military and security matters; in the South, militarization, the rise of nationalism, conflicts between TNCs and nation-states, and conflicts between international public organizations and the sovereignty of states. Notwithstanding the complexity of these issues, change in the next 100 years will be more profound than the already deep-seated changes which occurred in the past century. Attempts to foster the NIEO will make change less chaotic, while attempts to block it will not prevent change from occurring.

Vladislav Tikhomirov, using the conceptual tools of systems analysis, makes a basic distinction between a system of elements (or actors) in the world economy, and a system of relationships between the elements. The NIEO concerns primarily the system of relations between the world capitalist system and the economic system of the Third World. Thus the difficulties experienced by Third World countries are the result of a deep crisis of the world capitalist system. There is no interdependence in the relationship between the capitalist countries and the Third World on the one hand, the Third World and the socialist system on the other. As actors or elements in the world system, socialist countries support the NIEO in principle, because they are interested in a stable system based on equality, justice and mutual benefit. In their view conditions in developing countries can be improved first of all through domestic social and economic reform, and by restructuring economic relations with the capitalist countries. The latter must acquire a legal and institutional, rather than a purely commercial character, because the most important issues of the NIEO are, in fact, legal and political in nature.

Since the binding and enforceable nature of the new order is one of the most difficult yet important issues in the NIEO negotiations, the concluding paper, by K. Venkata Raman, acquires particular significance. International law must evolve to meet the challenge that awaits it in the international economic sphere. Its very foundations are challenged, since the present laissez-faire international economic system has traditionally based much of its authority upon it. Legal concepts which work well in local or domestic contexts (private ownership, contract, corporate personality) present major impediments when transplanted into the international instruments of the NIEO. The majority of developing countries view the NIEO as a demand for changing the basis of international law but shy away from using it to justify their claims, lacking an adequate definition of the substance of the new concepts. These difficulties beset the negotiation of such diverse issues as Third World debt, technical and financial aid, the transfer of technology, the most favored nation clause, tariff and non-tariff barriers, invisible trade, the formation of producers' associations, access to markets through regulating the monopoly practices of TNCs, restrictive business practices, the principle of permanent sovereignty over natural resources, and the free choice of domestic political and economic systems. A careful specification of policies is needed, together with the formulation of the content of the entailed legal obligations and the definition of the situations to which they apply. Since the latter are too various to admit adequate definition, a system of objective and dependable third-party settlement must be worked out. A U.N. convention on direct foreign investment could provide a framework in which such settlements could be achieved. If it elaborates the principles of international law in this sphere, it would encourage TNCs to undertake technology transfers, redeployment of industrial production sites, and new investment in developing countries, while enabling developing countries to unfold their capacities in shipping, insurance, transportation, and marketing. It would also provide a basis for the renegotiation of existing contractual or concessionary arrangements between host country governments and TNCs.

In Part One the present volume presents some important perspectives on the structure of the world economy; in Part Two it relates the principles of the NIEO to the real-world structures which they must modify or supplant. Political, institutional, and legal considerations emerge as key elements in the orderly establishment of a new international economic order, notwithstanding the economic substance of the objectives.

In closing this brief introduction it may be worth repeating that, as the authors of this volume demonstrate, the NIEO is not a set of temporary demands by a group of dissatisfied countries; it is a timely policy initiative universally needed to amend existing imbalances and growing inequities of the current world economy, in the name of economic as well as social justice and equity, and in the interest of all members of the human community. Whatever the disagreements and conflicts on particular points, if the historic and humanistic significance of the NIEO is upheld, there will be a new surge of courage, initiative, solidarity, and goodwill to accompany the long months and years of negotiations, and the decades of careful yet hopefully bold implementation, that will be required to translate the NIEO from a set of principles and resolutions into economic and social reality.

I
Perspectives on the Structure of the World Economy

1 The Structure of the World Economy: A Northern Perspective*

Michael Hudson, New York

A BROAD HISTORICAL PERSPECTIVE

International trade prior to 1945 was conducted by essentially self-sufficient nations, producing exportable surpluses of certain products over and above their own needs. Countries traded because it seemed more efficient to do so than to produce at home the goods available less expensively from abroad. International commerce thus remained an option of buying from the cheapest market, not a life or death necessity. Established trade patterns were still characterized by flexibility rather than dependency.

International borrowing and investment were also voluntary. Countries rarely had to borrow in order to avoid default on their foreign debts, except in the case of war-related indebtedness. Borrowing was normally for self-amortizing projects which, over time, enabled countries to repay their debts with interest. With the exception of war-related transfers of capital, international payments did not fall very far out of balance.

In short, the world economy possessed a degree of voluntariness and flexibility that has now been lost. Today's structural rigidities did not yet exist, nor were they anticipated.

Export surpluses fell into four categories. The first consisted of naturally endowed nonrenewable minerals such as tin, copper, oil, and iron. The second category also represented primary commodities, in the form of renewable agricultural products such as spices and coffee, cotton and rubber, grains and peanuts (climate and other geographic factors seemed naturally to favor some regions in the production of

*The three papers in Part One were originally presented at an international meeting in Mexico, in January 1979, under the titles:
Structural Imbalances in the World Economy (Michael Hudson)
A View of North-South Relations (Aldo Ferrer)
Contradictions in the Quest for a New International Economic Order (Oteiza Fontanals, Porta and Schkolnik)

3

these commodities). The third export category comprised clothing, steel, and other basic industrial manufactures. Finally, a fourth category has emerged in the form of high-technology or "information-intensive" manufactures, in which innovation rates are quite high. These products require comparatively massive research and development investment, government subsidy, and worldwide marketing facilities in order to break even. Examples include arms, aircraft, computers, and communications equipment.

The two industrial categories are characterized by acquired rather than "natural" advantage. They developed as a result of active and prescient policy planning, and a relatively high degree of protectionism. Most important, they have been concentrated in temperate zone nations which seemed least endowed with natural resources at the outset of the great European economic transformation that followed discovery of the New World some five centuries ago.

Industrial capability first developed in the richest agricultural countries, such as India and Italy which enjoyed comparatively warm climates and fertile soils. These were the countries which first accumulated an economic surplus, in the form of food output able to support a commercial and urban population. Over time, however, manufactured goods have come to be produced mainly by temperate zone nations. Despite the fact that these nations entered the modern industrial epoch with the fewest apparent natural advantages, they have acquired a growing degree of technological sophistication, and have created a highly skilled and well-paid labor force, a far-reaching urban and social infrastructure, and an abundance of liquid investment capital that has been channeled through increasingly sophisticated capital and money markets. In recent years, as their agriculture has been industrialized and commercialized into what is now termed agribusiness, they have acquired a growing food-exporting capability. Northern Europe and North America have thus become major food exporters as well as the leading industrial nations. Instead of becoming dependent on countries more liberally endowed with precious raw materials and with original or natural agricultural advantages, the industrial nations have become economically self-sufficient and independent.

Meanwhile, the regions which seemed five centuries ago to possess the best long-term growth prospects have now fallen into a state of economic dependence. They entered the industrial epoch with what seemed to be the broadest range of economic options before them. Yet, they have fallen into so deep a state of dependence that broad sectors of their populations are threatened with technologically spurred unemployment and economic obsolescence. Their natural agricultural advantages do not enable them to compete with the acquired advantages of capital-intensive food production and marketing methods employed in the leading industrial nations. Although today's less developed countries remain predominantly agricultural, many have fallen into severe food deficits. Although their per capita energy consumption is far lower than in the high-productivity and high-wage industrial economies, fuel represents the second major factor in their chronic trade deficits.   Despite their relative poverty, they are already insolvent on international accounts, and they continue to run deeper and deeper into debt as overdue interest and amortization payments pile up on their existing borrowings. In short, their economic future seems cloudy. They have lost many economic, financial, technological, and international options, while the industrial nations enjoy a relatively broad range of them.

This situation was not decreed by nature. It was created by nations moving to acquire industrial advantages through active trade and development strategies, and by translating these advantages into control of world markets and resources through colonization, foreign investment, and military conquest. Having secured these economic advantages, the temperate zone nations have consolidated their power by reinforcing an inequitable status quo. This status quo is taken for granted by today's "scientific" and "positive" mathematical models, which project historical trends as if they were natural and permanent. And yet these trends now threaten to divide the world into two economically distinct layers. If sustained, they will polarize the international economy between rich, Northern, diversified, self-sufficient economies and poor, Southern, export monocultures.

How did this division come about? Initially, the world economy was fractured by financial strains rather than by trade dislocations. These financial strains occurred among the industrial nations themselves rather than between North and South. World War I left a legacy of German reparations and inter-Ally arms debts far beyond the ability of Europe's debtor countries to pay. By 1931 the system of world payments based on these reparations and war debts broke down, leaving a financial crisis in its wake that brought on the Great Depression of the 1930s.

The economic depression hit less developed countries especially hard. Their government revenues had become increasingly dependent on taxes and royalties levied on raw materials exports, whose prices and sales volume fell sharply. Governments in raw materials exporting countries simply printed money to finance their budget deficits; the alternative would have been to cut back federal spending programs to a point threatening economic and political instability.

World War II seemed to restabilize international trade and payments for these countries. Nearly all nations showed themselves able to satisfy their domestic food requirements and other essential needs during the wars that interrupted world trade prior to 1945. Indeed, their enforced economic isolation spurred rather than hampered their economic diversification and development. Less developed countries were obliged to produce at home the food and manufactured goods they could no longer obtain from their traditional suppliers. And while they diversified their economies, their wartime shipment of raw materials to the belligerent powers enabled them to accumulate foreign exchange in the form of sterling and dollar balances.

These foreign exchange holdings promised to finance their postwar economic development. In 1946 a new cosmopolitan era thus seemed to be at hand. The major problem seemed to be the threat of depression in Europe and North America as they shifted from wartime production to a peacetime economy. Europe's gold had been drained to the United States prior to the war, and continued to flow to the United States during the late 1940s. This was why Marshall Plan aid and other concessionary grants were extended to European industrial nations – to bolster their postwar reconstruction and, in the process, sustain their demand for American exports.

Economic expansion in North America and Europe was expected to spur demand for world raw materials, and thus to provide income for less developed countries to modernize their economies. A development pattern, chiefly oriented toward exports was supposed to enable them to create a competitive economic and social infrastructure, and thus to meet more and more of their own needs. Many economists, therefore, expected low-income countries to begin catching up with the industrial high-income countries. Economic "latecomers" were expected to skip over intermediate stages of technological and social development. An epoch that would be free of war, poverty, and dependency was widely anticipated. Free international trade and an open door to international investment were supposed to spur world demand for Third World labor employed in the export sector, which, by a kind of economic osmosis, was supposed to bolster wage levels and employment in the domestic economies as well.

Japan seemed to exemplify this principle. It exported products of low-wage labor, and invested its trade surpluses in high-productivity capital to steadily increase its productive powers over time. If other Asian, Latin American, and African countries had followed suit, a new era of interdependent world prosperity might indeed have occurred.

THE PRESENT SITUATION

What has actually occurred is that world dependence, poverty, and armaments have reached unparalleled proportions during the past 35 years. Less developed countries have become increasingly dependent on the high-productivity industrial nations for their grains as well as for their consumer goods, replacement parts, arms, and machinery. While agricultural and industrial productivity has surged in the North, it has stagnated in the South. Indeed, productivity in the industrial nations has risen even more rapidly than wage levels and living standards, enabling high-wage labor to undersell low-wage Third World labor by a widening margin when adjusted for a unit-cost basis. In economic jargon, the Third World's factoral (that is, productivity-adjusted) terms of trade have deteriorated much more seriously than its commodity terms of trade. Third World countries have been able to export only their nonrenewable resources, at prices that do not reflect long-term replacement costs. They have parted with their "natural" mineral endowment to pay for renewable agricultural and industrial consumer goods and arms that find no counterpart in a buildup of future income-earning capital. They have run into debt to pay for these commodities, and are thus living off their past at the expense of their future. And they have been advised to do so by industrial country governments and economists who have told them that all this is in their best interest!

By 1952, the much feared postwar depression had not occurred in the North. Both Europe and North America had successfully rechanneled their productive capacity for a prosperous peace. But economic conditions remained stagnant in the South. Raw materials exporters did not embark upon the self-financing growth in living standards and productive powers that was achieved by the successfully diversified economies. They deteriorated into the position of export monocultures, a situation which was only aggravated by the Korean War boom in commodity prices during 1950-51. Third World Countries did not share in the great quarter-century of postwar prosperity (1945-70) to anywhere near the extent enjoyed by the industrial nations. Their labor and soil productivity grew much more slowly, and their incomes shrank as a proportion of the world total. Living standards for most of their populations declined as their rural exodus found little counterpart in productive industrial growth. Most of their nominal GNP growth reflected a proliferation of social-economic overhead and related cost functions (including arms purchases) that did not abet meaningful economic production.

Third World countries now find themselves confronted with widening productivity and cost gaps to be surmounted before they can achieve competitive status with the successfully industrialized nations. Closing of these productivity gaps requires a costly modernization of their labor productivity in agriculture, industry, and services; this in turn would require a massive government infrastructure investment. Unless these gaps can be closed, Third World countries face the prospect of becoming uncompetitive, and even economically obsolete in their own markets. Their poorly paid labor is less and less able to compete with the high-wage capital-intensive labor of the industrial nations; in fact, much of it threatens to take the form of a chronically unemployed social-overhead burden.

On balance, the compartmentalization of world production between Third World export economies and the leading industrial nations has worked to concentrate economic, technological, and social progress in the latter. The problem is that Third World "development" has been warped into self-defeating forms. Raw materials exports have declined relative to world trade as a whole. While the industrial nations have consolidated their technological progress by increasing their incomes and living standards – largely by running into debt – Third World countries have been forced to "live within their means," which are woefully inadequate to sustain the required growth in educational levels, health and welfare, domestic investment, and infrastructure spending needed to work their way out of poverty. They suffer from austerity programs imposed by the International Monetary Fund (IMF), while the industrial nations of the North manage to avoid pursuing this self-defeating policy.

The result is that Third World countries are unable to embark upon the self-sustaining pattern of growth that is the hallmark of true development. What has "developed" has been their dependency patterns, not their independence. What has grown has been their overhead and cost functions, not their net productive powers.

Matters became more serious during the recession conditions of the 1970s. Just as the developing countries bore the brunt of world recession in the 1930s, so today their falling export and tax revenues are spurring inflationary money creation stemming from their untenable balance-of-payments positions. While world demand for raw materials falls off, their need to purchase food, replacement parts, and other essentials from the industrial nations has grown.

The industrial nations, on the other hand, have reacted to depression conditions by raising their trade barriers and inaugurating a new protectionism. Third World governments respond to their balance-of-payments deficits by simply printing money to finance their domestic spending. The alternative is to cut back programs so far as to trigger political instability and economic collapse. Thus, world recession is once again proving to be highly inflationary for most of the Third World countries. Their foreign currency values are collapsing to reflect their adverse balance of trade and payments. This is spurring a general capital flight which strips them even of their modest present investment resources. Their economic depression is aggravated all the more as their savings and investment functions are translocated to the industrial nations.

For the industrial nations, Third World development connotes precisely an increased "interdependence" that all too often has meant dependence. It represents a situation in which Third World countries specialize in those types of production that the industrial nations elect not to produce themselves, in particular raw materials resource extraction and low-wage, labor-intensive manufactures. It implies an emphasis on export production rather than on domestic economic development, and, specifically, a monoculture syndrome rather than economic diversification. This lopsided export-oriented underdevelopment pattern has contributed to the fact that many Third World exports are sold near their low-cost margin of production, in exchange for industrial-nation manufactures and food sold at their high-cost margin. Thus, the profit and capital accumulation functions have been concentrated in exports from the North (recently joined by petroleum exports), not in exports of the countries of the South, in which most of the world's population is concentrated.

These structural problems stem essentially from three major syndromes that distinguish Third World development from that enjoyed by the Northern economies. These three syndromes are the monoculture syndrome; the debtor syndrome, which involves financial insolvency on international accounts; and the austerity (or poverty) syndrome, which results from the need to submit to IMF austerity programs and thereby forgo the economy-of-high-wages principle that has supported economic development in all of today's industrial nations.

THREE OBSTACLES TO FURTHER DEVELOPMENT

The Monoculture Syndrome

The monoculture syndrome represents an attempt to develop by export-oriented rather than by domestic investment, and by narrowing rather than expanding the Third World's range of economic options. It is the opposite of economic diversification and self-sufficiency. As its name indicates, it involves a specialization of exports, which rarely are absolute necessities to the industrial consumer nations in view of the wide range of alternative supplies that have come into being.

One of the most obvious problems of this development pattern is the fact that most raw materials face what economists call "inelastic" world demand (a situation in which price fluctuations exceed change in quantity). For instance, in a harvest failure the price of grain or coffee rises by more than the volume declines, so that farmers may actually benefit. When OPEC governments reduced oil exports, price increases more than compensated. Conversely, in the case of a good harvest, the price may fall by more than the volume of output increases, reducing net income accordingly. This suggests that when Third World countries seek to balance their international payments by exporting more of their traditional monoculture raw materials, their export revenues may well decline. The more they sell, the less they earn. In this respect Third World "development" has been channeled into a self-defeating form. Raw materials exporters have been led to compete with each other rather than with the industrial nations on which they have become increasingly dependent for food and other necessities.

The monoculture syndrome has come to be associated with a dual-economy structure created by a high-productivity economy increasingly segregated from the domestic economy. Although this export sector seems, in itself, to be a net benefit to the economy to the extent that it provides government foreign exchange revenues to sustain the growing trade and payments deficits of the subsistence and government sectors, its political and economic consequences actually retard domestic development. (This was, after all, a main reason why the United States fought its Civil War in 1861-65: in order to free the North from the impeding backwardness of the South and its free trade slave economy.)

The more resources are devoted to monoculture exports, the more domestic agriculture and other sectors are retarded. Government infrastructure spending is devoted to building up the export sector, not the domestic subsistence sector. The export sector seems to be earning much more gross revenue, but it is burdened with many balance-of-payments leakages. Most of these leakages stem from foreign ownership, in the form of remitted earnings, patent and licensing fees and other service payments, wages for foreign management personnel, imports of capital equipment used in producing exports, international shipping and insurance costs, warehousing and brokerage fees, and debt-service on the foreign loans undertaken to finance the export infrastructure. Over and above these direct leakages are the indirect "opportunity costs" (that is, lost opportunities) of not using potentially available investment resources to replace imports. The domestic subsistence sector is permitted to languish. (The classical example is afforded by Chile, whose growth in copper exports since the 1950s has been totally offset by rising food import costs. By concentrating on copper production rather than modernizing its own agriculture, Chile has run into debt, lost millions of tons of its natural endowment of copper ore, and has limited its options accordingly. In effect, its foreign-owned export sector has subsidized its dependency — and made it all the more difficult to break out of its now established dependency pattern.)

These patterns result in a growing international dependence, especially on food and other necessary imports. This occurs when minimum necessary (or "break-even") consumption of food and other products exceeds normal domestic supply. The balance must be imported. This is the foundation of the structural trade deficits faced by Third World countries. On the one hand their monoculture syndrome imposes a structural limit on their maximum export earnings: attempts to export a larger quantity of raw materials work to reduce their prices by an amount that more than offsets the increased sales volume, thereby diminishing the net sales revenue. Meanwhile, growing collective Third World dependence on food and other industrial nation exports works to bid up their prices, enabling the industrial nations to cover the costs of their own high-wage labor and the capital accumulation costs associated with these exports. Dependence results when imports for the Third World become a matter of absolute necessity — for instance, to avoid starvation or to keep the economy from breaking down for lack of essential replacement parts and other products — rather than merely an exercise of economic choice by buying in the cheapest market.

Many Third World countries have the needed agricultural labor and land, but this sector has often fallen into a state of economic obsolescence. It cannot compete with the high-productivity capital and high-wage labor of the industrial nations, even at a subsistence wage rate. The human body is not as efficient at converting food energy into physical energy or basic servomechanism tasks as today's power-driven machines are at converting fuels; but even the lowest paid worker costs more to support than it costs to buy and operate machinery to perform the same production tasks. Thus, under free trade, Third World countries cannot economically pursue an "appropriate technology" strategy. Substitution of labor for capital — especially under conditions where the food necessary to support this labor is priced at the high-cost international margin — is not economically efficient in terms of market norms. It can be made to appear efficient only by protective tariffs or domestic subsidy. And these are precisely the policies being denied by the IMF and northern aid-lending governments, which have gained an increasing authority over Third World policies by virtue of the latter's international insolvency.

The Debtor Syndrome

Third World economic dependence has led to structural balance-of-payments deficits and insolvency. Unable to satisfy its growing food needs and its domestic demand for other consumer goods and services, the Third World is obliged to import these products. However, the costs of these imports are not covered by export earnings, except in a few oil-rich countries since 1973. The resulting trade deficit must be financed by borrowing. Third World countries have borrowed and borrowed, with neither their own governments nor those of their creditor nations bothering to analyze just how these debts can be repaid, or what the economic consequences of their repayment will be.

The fact is that the Third World's debt as a whole cannot be repaid, except by reducing its population to a form of utter servitude and sacrificing all hope of future development. Third World countries find themselves oppressed by a tyranny of debt. And orthodox economic theory diverts attention from analyzing its costs and consequences.

The first question to be asked is, how large is Third World debt-service relative to its capacity to pay? This question cannot be answered simply by computing debt-service (interest plus amortization) as a proportion of gross export revenues. As already mentioned, as much as one-third of nominal export revenues for Third World countries is retained abroad by the foreign owners of the minerals industry and other export sectors. Only the tax payments and domestic wage and materials costs are remitted to the host countries of foreign-owned, export-oriented investment. Thus, the first adjustment to be made consists of a computation of net export proceeds actually realized by Third World economies.

The second adjustment entails a computation of the net trade balance as a whole. After all, Third World export proceeds do not represent a freely available fund out of which debt-service can represent a first change. As discussed above, many imports are essential. If Third World populations find food import prices rising, they can hardly elect to eat less. They must either pay the higher prices or starve. If energy prices are rising, they face a similar dilemma: if they consume less, they create domestic bottlenecks that impair their capacity to produce. They also must buy replacement parts, and their societies have become dependent upon a given structural level of imports. The cost of these imports frequently exceeds their net export proceeds, even before meeting debt-service payments.

This untenable situation has obliged many Third World countries to borrow merely to finance their existing debts. They find themselves bereft of the resources needed to finance new investment capable of generating an economic surplus out of which to repay these debts. They are in fact in a position similar to that of Germany in the 1920s. Germany was obliged to make reparations payments far beyond its capacity to export, especially in the face of the trade barriers raised by the leading creditor nations. Some economists in the United States and Europe suggested that perhaps Germany could raise reparations funds by selling more to the Soviet Union, and indeed a moderate increase in German exports in this direction occurred. But this is not a viable option for today's Third World countries. The Communist bloc nations are themselves hoping to balance their international payments in part by exporting more to Third World countries.

In the 1920s, John Maynard Keynes insisted that creditor nations detail just how debtor-countries should extricate themselves from debt but the task proved to be beyond their capacity. The German economy collapsed, followed by that of the European Allies, and finally of the United States itself. Today, the world economy is once again in danger of such a collapse. No attempt has been made to explain how Third World countries can export goods to the creditor nations, collectively or individually, to service their outstanding debts.

In order to service these debts, Third World countries must export more. But this puts downward price pressure on their terms of trade. They must exchange more of their commodities, and more of their currency, for creditor nation currency (in addition to buying more creditor nation food and other exports to sustain their growing populations). This leads to currency depreciation under today's system of floating (or, more accurately, sinking) exchange rates. This in turn impairs their domestic investment functions, making it even more difficult for them to generate an exportable surplus.

The resulting dilemma threatens to engulf both Third World and industrial countries. Not only is much of the Third World's recent debt accumulation the result of recession conditions in the industrial nations, but it has become a major factor aggravating this recession. Lower Third World export prices and exhausted credit lines are impairing Third World demand for industrial nation exports. The lack of credit-worthiness of many of the most seriously affected countries has resulted in a write-down of the value of commercial bank assets and government loans in the industrial nations, impairing the power of the latter to create credit.

Matters are aggravated by the fact that much of the Third World's debt was contracted when its export prices were higher than they are today in real purchasing power terms. This is partly because prices for Third World imports of food, energy, and other necessities were relatively much lower before 1973. Thus, much more of their domestic labor and capital is required to pay off this debt. The Third World's net export-earning capacity is made even more problematic by its need to continue to buy food and oil on world markets merely to meet break-even costs. In reality, Third World economies are operating in a net deficit position on international account. Many countries are obliged to sell their raw materials at less than replacement costs (e.g., at the high-cost margin) in order to live in the present. The terminus of this process will be to strip their economies of their mineral endowments, at which point they will collapse from within.

Matters are made even more inequitable by today's system of international finance, that is, by the U.S. Treasury bill standard. Third World foreign exchange reserves are held in the form of loans to industrial key-currency nations, in particular the United States. And holding central bank reserves in the form of U.S. Treasury bills represents a de facto transfer of savings from Third World countries to the United States.

This inequitable central bank transfer is further aggravated by the fact that the international value of the U.S. dollar has fallen sharply against the value of the leading European and Asian currencies. Furthermore, a large portion of the U.S. domestic purchasing power of the dollar has also been eroded by inflationary pressures. This inflation and currency depreciation constitutes the path of least resistance for key-currency nations to solve their own internal economic and political problems. But this process exacerbates problems for countries holding their international monetary reserves in the form of dollars and other depreciating currencies.

Special Drawing Rights (SDRs) were developed to supplant the dollar in world finance. But they were introduced mainly to alleviate the balance-of-payments deficits of the industrial nations, and in particular to conserve the gold stock of the United States. They were handed out in proportion to existing IMF quotas, which reflect existing world disparities in international reserves rather than degrees of economic need. Thus, the United States and Europe have received the lion's share of SDRs. A modest portion of the profits earned by the industrial gold-holding nations as a result of gold revaluation since 1971 has been turned over to Third World countries in the forms of SDRs. But the amount is only a token.

SDRs are granted by the IMF, whose economists have increasingly taken over both international and domestic policy making for Third World debtor countries. This extension of IMF authority has resulted from the Third World's need to borrow abroad to cover its trade deficits while servicing its mounting debt burden. Foreign governments and commercial banks have become increasingly reluctant to extend new loans except as part of a package agreement associated with IMF "surveillance" programs. These programs impose an economic and financial austerity on Third World countries that is directly opposed to the nature of today's diversified industrial economies.

Third World countries have suffered from the growing protectionism and self-interest of current aid lending. This aid has been given increasingly on terms that benefit the lending rather than the recipient countries. This is especially the case with bilateral aid. For instance, in the case of U.S. nonmilitary foreign aid the main flow of foreign exchange is from Third World countries to the U.S. Government. To be sure, the net flow of physical goods and services is from the United States. But U.S. aid is tied to goods and services produced at home, and to the relatively expensive use of U.S. ships to transport the aid-financed commodity sales. This aid must be repaid over time, with interest. It must be immediately paid for in domestic currency counterpart funds which are made available to the U.S. Government and its many agencies. Furthermore, it has involved guarantees that aid-borrowing governments will not develop their agricultural and other productive powers in directions that might compete with U.S. producers and exporters, especially in agriculture.

Matters are hardly better in the case of aid borrowing from multinational organizations, which are controlled by the industrial nations who put up most of the aid-loan funds. If Third World countries borrow from the World Bank, they are obliged to pursue an export-oriented, import-dependent philosophy of development. This has the effect of increasing the relative world oversupply of Third World raw materials, impairing export prices and foreign exchange earnings for the Third World as a whole.

Such aid works to increase the Third World's dependency on the industrial nations, not to improve its progress toward self-sufficiency. Under these conditions the question is raised as to how much aid the Third World can afford to obtain. Much of the aid, especially in food, has been to support its consumption functions rather than its production functions. Thus, it does not help aid-borrowing countries to repay their aid-related debts.

In any event, the industrial nations have reduced the proportion of their national income devoted to foreign aid. They have increasingly tied this aid to purchases of their own exports. Until now they have extended it in the form of loans rather than outright grants. Today's world recession, and the balance-of-payments pressures that confront many industrial nations, threaten to exacerbate these problems unless the now negotiated aid reforms and debt cancellations are speedily implemented.

Industrial nations may argue that resource transfers should take the form of trade rather than aid. But when they speak of trade they mean continued Third World emphasis on capital-intensive mineral production or on low-wage manufactures which threaten to exert further downward pressure on Third World terms of trade.

The Austerity Syndrome

The austerity syndrome which underlies IMF monetary philosophy is the financial counterpart to the monoculture syndrome. It is immediately responsible for the Third World's failure to develop. It rests on the perverse belief that the way to become prosperous in the long run is to become even poorer in the short run — as if this will not thwart rather than develop productive powers. It seeks to balance international payments by reducing income, in the false belief that this will reduce import demand rather than aggravate international dependence by discouraging domestic investment. The fact is that the output lost from foregone opportunities and impaired productivity exceeds the value of consumption and imports "saved" by wage reductions. Third World productive powers tend to fall even more sharply than consumption as a result of the strikes, political disorders, and changes of government that have become hallmarks of IMF "stabilization" programs. The impoverished state of Third World labor, and cutbacks in social-economic infrastructure spending, further aggravate matters. In short, IMF austerity programs aggravate rather than help matters. They block the economy-of-high-wages principle that has characterized economic development for all of today's successfully industrialized nations. It is therefore necessary to counterpose the economic and political impact of these two opposing philosophies of development.

Nearly all economic phenomena – those of decay and poverty as well as of growth and prosperity – are characterized by cumulative, positive-feedback systems. In the industrial nations, rising living standards have contributed to an even more rapid growth of productivity, to even higher trade and payments surpluses, to higher rates of domestic investment, and to more flexible and rapidly evolving social institutions. Rising living standards have fostered development of an increasingly educated and skilled labor force, whose wage rates have become factored into the price of industrial nation exports.

Third World countries, by contrast, suffer from a cumulative disequilibrium weighted downward. Their slower growth in living standards has retarded their accumulation of both human and material capital. They suffer from inadequate dietary standards and educational opportunities, and from depressed growth in domestic investment as a result of relatively slow market demand. Their economic momentum is not sufficient to transform their institutional rigidities. This is true especially of their land tenure systems, which continue to impede their growth in food-producing powers.

Matters are aggravated by the Third World's demographic overhead. Instead of discouraging population growth (as anticipated by Malthusian models), poverty spurs fertility rates. An increasing proportion of youth not yet in the labor force, and an increasingly urbanized and congested population without productive employment (much less export-oriented employment), must be fed and otherwise supported by "inelastic" food production and inadequate growth in fiscal resources. Widening trade deficits to support this population are financed largely by running into foreign debt, whose interest charges continue to rise to reflect the general world inflation. The Third World's minimum "break-even" or "structural" level of essential imports exceeds monoculture export earnings by a widening margin.

Even before the development of birth control devices, population growth was traditionally highest in countries with the lowest incomes (except for newly settled countries), and, within each country, was lowest for those classes with the highest incomes. This creates a cumulative feedback problem for low-income countries: not only must their meager domestic output be distributed over a rapidly growing population, but the investment needed to support this demographic growth is retarded by the limited internal market and external purchasing power.

All this represents the opposite of the Malthusian belief that higher income will reflect itself in more rapid population growth. It suggests that the long-term cure for rapid rates of population growth lies in sustaining higher living standards (along with a corresponding system of social and cultural values), rather than in imposing even stricter austerity.

Another demographic problem associated with economic austerity and monoculture production is the brain drain from Third World countries. Not only does much of the foreign-educated population remain abroad, but Third World adult labor emigrates in search of higher earning power and greater political freedom.

CONCLUSIONS

The above syndromes reinforce each other in imposing poverty, dependence, austerity, and technological obsolescence on Third World countries, which can no longer escape from their existing world price levels and marketing structures. Their labor, and even their land and mineral resources, have been rendered uncompetitive to the point where they threaten to become economically obsolete. Low-productivity Third World labor and land is thrown directly into competition with that of more technologically and economically advanced economies.

The result is a vicious spiral of poverty. On the one hand, the Third World's slower growth in living standards seems to be an inevitable consequence of its lower productivity levels. But these relatively low living standards, in turn, retard the rate of accumulation of human and material capital. Institutional rigidities, especially in the area of land reform, impede growth in food production. The resulting trade and payments deficit obliges Third World countries to borrow abroad, on increasingly onerous terms culminating in their enforced submission to IMF austerity programs. They are thus blocked from embarking upon the self-sustaining feedback process of growth that is, after all, the hallmark of development; they suffer an even greater dependence on more successfully industrialized economies whose expanding internal markets, higher investment, productivity growth, and other characteristics of cumulative economic development further widen world income and productivity differentials. Their foreign currency values sink to reflect their adverse balance of payments, which is increasingly eroded by the burden of debt-service. These developments spur a capital flight that strips Third World countries of potential investment resources; this in turn accelerates the translocation of world savings and investment to the industrial nations.

This international income and productivity maldistribution is a form of inequity. But the fact must be faced that it does indeed represent a form of economic "equilibrium," for underlying these income disparities are widening productivity disparities: the products of low-productivity, low-wage labor are exchanged for those of high-productivity, high-wage labor at deteriorating terms of trade.

Much of the Third World's borrowing was undertaken to develop its export sectors in ways which, directly or indirectly, retarded its agriculture and other import-competing sectors. Thus, the net result of foreign-aid and related borrowings has been to indebt Third World countries to the industrial nations while rendering them even more dependent for their food, arms, luxuries, and other consumer goods. They have grown financially dependent on their creditors to continue financing their trade dependence. As their trade and payments deficits have grown increasingly severe, they have been obliged to borrow more and more. Unable to repay their scheduled debt-service, they have been obliged to submit to austerity programs that further retard their growth of productive powers, infrastructure spending, and private investment. They thus become less and less able to balance their international trade and payments while servicing their mounting burden of debts. They find themselves in a quandary with, seemingly, no escape.

Economic theory has not prepared Third World countries for this state of affairs. Each country is supposed to produce what it is best at producing, under conditions in which reciprocal demand among countries enables each country's international payments to remain roughly in balance. "Macroeconomic" — that is, nonstructural — monetary and income adjustments are supposed to keep international trade in balance. But the degree of imbalance has now become critical rather than merely marginal. It far exceeds the ability of generalized money and income manipulations to cope with it. The problem has become structural.

2 The Structure of the World Economy: Southern Perspectives

I. Aldo Ferrer,
Buenos Aires
II. Enrique Oteiza,
Jorge Fontanals,
Fernando Porta,
Susana Scholnik,
Caracas

FROM AMERICAN HEGEMONY TO THE TRILATERAL SYSTEM

From the end of World War II to the beginning of the 1970s, two main periods can be recognized in the evolution of the world economic system. The first encompasses the years of overwhelming American hegemony; the second, emergence of the dominance of the trilateral group of the United States, Japan, and Western Europe. In the latter period, American hegemony was influenced by its interdependence with a group of highly powerful economies. The trilateral group had been developing throughout the first period and resulted directly from, among other things, the way in which the United States exercised its initial position of hegemony. (Given the limited weight of the socialist countries within the world economic system, it is logical to concentrate this analysis on the workings of the capitalist countries and the periphery associated with them. This restriction, therefore, applies to such expressions as world system or international order used in the text.)

After the war, America's production of goods and services represented more than 60 percent of total production in the capitalist industrial world; its gold reserves exceeded 80 percent of world reserves; and its exports accounted for nearly 30 percent of all exports from industrial countries. In the latter half of the 1940s, America's superiority to other industrial nations and the rest of the world was apparent both in trade and other current payments. Given the magnitude of the American economy, its overwhelming weight in the world system was not counteracted by similar outside influences on its own domestic system. This gave the American economy a considerable amount of autonomy in its external relations, and in the ability to conduct these relations independently from the administration of internal demand, liquidity, production, and employment. This autonomy was reinforced by the United States' dominance in the main assets of international reserve, and, consequently, by its ability to finance its

18

balance-of-payments deficits until well into the 1960s, without sub-stantially decreasing its gold reserves.

American economic assistance, through the Marshall Plan and other channels, played an important role in the postwar rebuilding of the main European countries and Japan. But much more than this direct aid, the dominant factor in the economic expansion of the system was America's commercial and financial relations with the other industrial countries. The traditional superiority of the United States was more than counter-balanced by the costs of financing its military and political influence on the rest of the world, and the growing investments of American companies abroad. This persistent deficit in the balance of payments was made up for primarily by an increase in the dollar holdings of the rest of the world. The subsequent increase in the other developed countries' international reserves speeded up the expansion of their consumption and internal liquidity, which allowed at the same time for the lifting of foreign trade and exchange restrictions inherited from the postwar period. Toward the end of the 1950s, the lifting of exchange restrictions for the main European currencies and the yen, and the reduction in tariffs and other trade restrictions, were accomplished through negotiations under the auspices of the General Agreement on Tariffs and Trade (GATT).

The recovery of Europe and Japan and the overvaluation of the dollar began to undermine the competitive position of the United States. Thus, a progressive weakening of the United States' commercial superiority was added to the deficits in the capital account and military expenses abroad. However, the reduction of the importance of the foreign sector, and the financing of the deficit through short-term loans, enabled the deterioration in the balance of payments to be suffered without having any noticeable effect on aggregate demand, production, or employment.

The American economy played a decisive role in the economic recovery of the industrialized world and in the vertiginous expansion of international trade. America's participation in this process was primar-ily achieved through its large industrial corporations and its main banks. Transnationalization was the main reason for the growth of the large industrial and financial enterprises of the United States. This process was primarily directed toward other industrial countries and thus further consolidated the ties within the developed world.

These trends brought about great changes in the structure of America's balance of payments. Alongside the continuing deterioration of the trade balance and the deficit in the capital account, the increasing presence of profits and shares of American investment overseas appeared as a partially compensatory factor. In other words, America's deterioration in trade and the deficit in its capital account was partially compensated for by its superiority in particular services, such as the sale of technology, and the return on American capital invested overseas.

The direction of the American economy, the expansion of its corporations, and the rapid growth of Europe and Japan gave impulse to a very rapid development in commercial transactions and in the movement of capital between the industrial countries. Thus, in but a few years a macromarket was created, embracing the main industrial economies within which the main currents of interchange were registered. The international division of labor, at the heart of the macromarket, was the dominant factor in the postwar economic experience. The old central-peripheral relationship, and the traditional division of labor between industrial societies and economies of primary production, were replaced by a similar relationship between industrial countries as dynamic nuclei of trade and the international movement of capital. Between 1948 and 1970, trade within the bloc of industrial nations rose from 64 to 77 percent of the total foreign trade of these countries. In the case of the United States, the increase (from 41 to 73 percent) was even more pronounced. The international division of labor in the developed world took place primarily in industrial production, and trade of manufactured goods between industrialized countries rose from 20 percent in the 1930s, to 31 percent in the 1960s and 42 percent in 1970.

On the other hand, central-peripheral trade quickly lost importance. In the 1930s it accounted for over 40 percent of world trade; by 1960 it had dropped to 32 percent and by 1970 to 27 percent. Of particular significance was the decline in Latin America's importance in the foreign trade of the United States. In relation to total imports, those from Latin America decreased from 35 to 11 percent between 1948 and 1970.

This process was influenced by a variety of factors linked to technical progress and changes in the nature of demand. The concentration of technical progress in capital-intensive industries, generators of economies susceptible to specialization on a world scale, promoted industrial development in the more complex sectors. Simultaneously, expansion was integrated into the context of the capitalist macromarket. American corporations played a decisive role in this integration of industrial economies and in the spread of technical progress. Even in Japan, where direct access to private investment from abroad was severely restricted, American technology contributed to rapid industrial development.

Low income-elasticity of demand for primary products was another decisive factor in the substantial change which took place in international trade, and in the share industrial and developing countries had within it. The decline in the importance of raw materials and foodstuffs in the overall expenditure of the advanced economies, the replacement of natural products by synthetics, and the reduction in the quantities of materials needed to make the final product, resulted in a relatively slow growth in the demand for primary products. To this was added the protectionist attitudes of the main countries towards domestic primary products. Trade between industrialized nations came to represent the largest proportion of world trade in foodstuffs and raw materials. Only some minerals, and oil in particular, escaped these trends in postwar world trade. This resulted in a rapid decline in the importance of primary products in world trade and a subsequent decrease in the peripheral nations' participation in this trade: from 30 percent in the late 1940s to 21 percent in 1960 and 17 percent in 1970.

The creation of the trilateral macromarket and the rapid expansion of transactions within it acted as powerful stimulants, particularly outside the United States. In continental economies, such as that of North America, internal factors followed suit, thus determining the rhythm and direction of development. However, in the rest of the industrial world, foreign trade jeopardized growing sectors of the economic system, particularly in the dynamic industries with fast expansion rates and high increase in productivity.

A variety of forces caused the growth of the American economy to be less forceful than that of Germany, Japan, and other industrialized countries until nearly the end of the 1960s. In the first place, the rapid rebuilding of the countries damaged by World War II enabled them to escape America's supremacy, which was based on the destruction of economic power in other industrialized countries. As a result, the industrial and technological residues left to these countries opened up new opportunities. Furthermore, economies of scale and specialization had more impact in Europe and Japan than in the United States. In the latter, the existence of a continental market and the advances which had already been achieved by the formation of large companies and conglomerates anticipated the increase in productivity (which was only achieved by a few countries after the war). For the same reason, foreign opportunities acted as a more important stimulus to productivity in European countries and Japan than in the United States which, given its continental market, had already achieved a high level of specialization and internal division of labor.

On the other hand, the overvaluation of the dollar impaired the United States' competitive position. This deterioration was not caused by errors of management in the process of adjustment between the industrial countries. On the contrary, it was a necessary condition for the formation of a bloc of industrial countries, and for the expansion of the accumulation of capital, production, and employment within it.

The United States' smaller rate of growth, relative to that of Germany, Japan, and other industrial countries, gradually eroded its overwhelming position of hegemony. Toward the end of the 1960s, American production accounted for 47 percent of total production in the industrial world, as opposed to 60 percent some 20 years earlier. The United States retained substantial importance in the macromarket, but the growing weight of Germany, Japan, and other industrialized countries progressively changed the relative positions and the power structure of the bloc. Furthermore, the United States was losing its share of international trade. Other industrial countries acquired a greater relative importance in commercial transactions, and their own corporations started to share in the international movement of capital, thus breaking the near monopoly held by American companies in the immediate postwar period. The international monetary system operated with considerable efficiency during the whole period and helped to develop the expansive forces of the world economy. The Bretton Woods agreement anticipated a fixed yet adjustable parity system which, linked to policies of internal adjustment, would allow for an orderly working of international payments and liquidity. However, the key to expansion lay in the continuing deficit of the United States' balance of payments and the rapid rise of dollar reserves in the rest of the world. The dollar quickly replaced gold as the main reserve currency outside the United States and as a source of increased international liquidity. The American deficit, and the surpluses of Germany, Japan, and other industrial countries, indicated a basic disorder in the process of international adjustment. It was, however, these very disorders which gave impulse to the growth of the macromarket, production, and employment on an international scale. Thus, the responsibility for the disequilibria in international payments does not lie in the rigidities of the parity adjustment mechanism anticipated in Bretton Woods; nor does it lie in the supposed foolishness of the monetary and fiscal policies of the main countries.

On a world scale, the United States' balance of payments played the same role as the central bank when, in a national economy, it financed part of the expenses by monetary expansion. In the industrial countries, fiscal and monetary policies were based on the Keynesian criteria of creating aggregate demand though the financing of deficits in order to achieve full employment. Within the group of industrial countries, the United States' balance of payments deficit and the increase in its short term loans played exactly the same role as an increase in the money supply and aggregate demand. This implied the triumph of Keynesianism on an international scale. Central bankers and monetary experts, who are in the habit of confusing appearances and reality, may have thought that the problems lay in the subtleties of the rules of adjustment. In actuality, it was the explicit and implicit decisions of these countries that caused the disequilibrium.

Every participant in the process benefited from it. The United States did so because, as issuing country of the main international reserve currency, it was able to finance the expansion of its companies, and of its political and military influence, without any real transfer of resources. The rest of the industrial countries benefited because in this way they received an impulse to their aggregate demand and their international reserves which acted as powerful agents to expansion.

The development of Euro-markets was one of the most significant consequences of the increase in international liquidity in the hands of the private sector and the monetary authorities. The activities of transnational corporations created commercial and financial currents within each conglomerate, which carried much weight in the workings of the market. The creation of a great financial power, outside the control of the countries' individual monetary authorities, was the basis of a secondary expansion in international liquidity which in turn contributed to an increase in international transactions and intensified the speculative movement of capital. The internationalization of banks, above all that of the American banks, was one of the most important features in the process of the integration and transnationalization of the macromarket and its linking to the Third World periphery as well as the socialist countries.

These trends continued virtually without setback during the second half of the 1940s and all of the 1950s. The result was a growth in production, commerce, and the international movement of capital unprecedented in the history of the world economy. Policies were established which tended to place emphasis on full employment as the main objective; the importance of the public sector increased significantly; and real earnings rose impressively in the industrial world. Seen in perspective, the results of American postwar policy were spectacular. It reached the basic goals which it had set in terms of the strengthening and interdependence of the industrial countries and the rapid expansion of large American companies throughout the rest of the world. This was a help in the United States' political and military strategy vis-a-vis the Soviet Union. The Vietnam War was the only serious setback in American policy, and it occurred in an area of marginal importance to the postwar economic system.

During this time of new, expansive currents in the international economy, the periphery remained peripheral. It was trapped in a vicious circle: specialization in the export of primary goods and growth in its demand for manufactured goods. The consequences were a decline in the relative importance of international trade in its economy and a chronic external disequilibrium. This process, which particularly reflects the experience of the greater part of Latin America, contributed to import substitution and industrialization. This new link with the industrialized world was formed by means of an increase in private investment in the industrial sector, the transfer of technology, and the establishment of more complex financial relations. To a large extent, the periphery was stimulated by the expansion of the capitalistic macromarket, thus creating new and more intimate links which were in turn growth-creating factors but, at the same time, obstacles to a faster, integrated, autonomous development.

During the 1960s, tensions within the American system began to increase. With the conclusion of the reconstruction of the European countries and Japan, and the consolidation of their development and position in international finance, the rest of the world began to oppose the continuing financing of American expansion through increased dollar holdings. Primarily, it was a question of reformulating the power structure within the macromarket, now that the United States' support was no longer essential to the reconstruction and launching processes. The United States' handling of political and military relations with the rest of the world was also brought into question, as was the international expansion of its corporations.

The political conflict was initiated by France. The growing disequilibrium in international payments was beginning to cause increasingly serious upheavals in the exchange markets. The conversion, by France and other countries, of part of their dollar holdings into gold from the United States Treasury rapidly undermined the guarantees of the short-term foreign loans of the United States.

On the other hand, the overvaluation of the dollar and the huge amounts of liquid capital existing in the international financial markets generated increases in speculative trends against the dollar, in anticipation of readjustment of its parity. From the first crisis in the London gold market until the beginning of the 1970s, the foreign exchange markets often suffered such intolerable tensions that they had to temporarily shut down.

The adjustment process of payment disequilibrium became the dominant theme in the international economic debate. At the same time, the desired equilibrium in the United States' balance of payments, along with a rapid decline in the importance of gold as a source of expansion of international liquidity, encouraged the search for alternatives to the dollar and gold. The first outcome of the IMF debates on the reform of the international monetary system was the establishment of special drawing rights in 1967.

During the 1960s all efforts to maintain the established rules of the game were unfruitful. The separation of the gold market from official holdings, the "swaps" and agreements between central banks in order to prop up the dollar and other currencies in difficulties, as well as the slight revaluation of the German mark, the yen, and other stronger currencies – all these attempts were totally inadequate in restoring equilibrium to international payments, creating a well ordered system of foreign exchange, or stimulating a moderate growth in international liquidity. The disequilibrium that followed America's attempts to impose a tax on interests in order to reverse the flow of short-term capital proved intolerably costly in terms of the domestic level of economic activity and employment. During this whole period, the maintenance of parity and convertibility of the dollar remained the basic goal of U.S. policy. This introduced a great rigidity into the system in which payment disequilibria and speculative movements of capital became exaggeratedly high.

The debate among the main countries centered on the fundamental problem of how to eliminate the American balance-of-payments deficit, and the surpluses of countries such as Germany and Japan. In the 1960s two main lines of argument developed. One of these, originating in France, stressed the need for the United States to balance its capital account and reduce its spending on military and political objectives overseas. This viewpoint emphasized the fact that the U.S. trade balance was still registering a surplus so that income from American investment overseas was still increasing. Equilibrium had to be restored in other areas of the balance of payments.

In contrast, the United States argued for adjustment through creating an increase in its trade surplus, which in its view was greatly restricted by the protectionist policies of some industrial nations – as in the case of the agricultural policy of the Common Market – and by resistance to the revaluation of its own currencies in relation to the dollar. These arguments continued to be made until August 1971. At that time President Nixon's measures brought about radical change in America's position in relation to the defense of the dollar's parity and convertibility, causing fundamental change in the existing rules of the game.

One must remember, however, that these controversies between industrial countries in no way jeopardized the common direction and interdependence they established after the war. But, in the framework of this new situation of diffused power in the trilateral system, these conflicts caused new repercussions when the United States, departing from its original position of hegemony, was lead to make compromises both for its own good and for the good of all others in this system.

During this entire period the periphery followed events passively and expectantly. The debates on the reform of the international monetary system and the agreements between the main nations within the "Group of Ten" and the Organization for Economic Cooperation and Development (OECD) gave only cursory notice to the problems facing developing nations. "Foreign aid," generalized preferences, and other schemes were mere palliatives, intended only to calm the growing political pressures of the periphery on the system.

From the beginning of the 1970s, tensions in the trilateral system began to mount. On the one hand, disequilibria in the international payments of the main industrial countries worsened, causing unbearable tensions in the international monetary system set up in Bretton Woods. On the other hand, the sharp increase in oil prices at the end of 1973 introduced a new and serious factor of disequilibrium in international payments. Much more than these factors, however, the crisis in the trilateral system was linked to the increase in inflationary pressures in developed countries and the inability to reconcile full employment with an acceptable price stability.

Faced with these new problems, postwar economic policies were challenged, and neoclassical and monetary orthodoxy began to acquire growing importance in the handling of economic policies. The control of inflation became the primary objective, even at the expense of growth and employment. At the same time, studies were made in the industrial world in which the material limits of long-term world development were discussed, in recognition of the shortages of exhaustible natural resources and of environmental pollution. This viewpoint was strengthened by the sudden rise in the price of oil and other primary products, and gave rise to proposals for the decelerating and eventual halting of growth. Demographic pressures in parts of the Third World and the resulting trends in population growth inspired cataclysmic visions of the future of mankind. However, the fatalism of some of these visions was dispelled by the results of demographic policies in certain countries, by the impact of better living standards as regulating agents in population growth, and by a more realistic appraisal of the availability of exhaustible natural resources. And in view of, above all, problems of recession, inflation, and unemployment, the attraction of long-term futuristic visions diminished in the developed countries as doubts of their reliability arose.

At the beginning of the 1970s the tensions within the trilateral system and the disequilibria in payments occurred in a framework of increasing production, employment, and international trade. But as of the 1973-74 recession, these tensions and imbalances took place in the context of slow growth, high unemployment, and persistent inflationary pressure. Consequently the readjustment of international payments became more difficult. There was an upsurge of protectionist demands which threatened the order in which the postwar macrocapitalist system had its roots. The system became less able to assimilate changes in the structure of production and external payments of its members, particularly in the case of the United States. This led to pronounced instability in the exchange markets, and in the value of the dollar and other main currencies; this in turn aggravated tensions and impeded the process of readjustment.

On the other hand the trilateral system faced new challenges from its periphery. The most significant of these was the increase in the price of oil. But the challenge exceeds even this, and is now reflected in proposals to restructure the entire international economic order and review traditional center-periphery relations. Although these relations are marginal to the fundamental interests of the trilateral system, they nevertheless aggravate the tensions under which it labors. Therefore, the main industrial countries now place greater importance in principle on their relations with the Third World. The seriousness of the trilateral system's position is not rooted in a simple crisis in international payments and adjustment of monetary instability. It now embraces a whole new plane encompassing the very dynamism of income distribution, growth, and employment in the industrialized world. Consequently the social bases on which the expansion of the industrial countries must occur to efficiently solve the problems of international economic relations seems unlikely unless a new basis can be found to maintain sustained growth in accumulation, production, and employment. This implies the discovery of valid strategies with which to grapple with conflicts in the distribution of power and income in the central economies – conflicts at the root of their current problems. In relation to economic policy it implies finding new guidelines in order to overcome the limitations of Keynesianism and of neoclassical and monetary orthodoxy, whose consequences are extremely costly in terms of price levels, production, and employment, and are moreover a threat to the survival of the liberal system of trade and balances on which the trilateral system was based, and by means of which its large corporations became transnational.

THE PRESENT INTERNATIONAL SITUATION AND ITS PROSPECTS

The crisis in the trilateral system had injurious effects on the periphery. Protectionism against imports from developing countries and a reduction in demand and prices aggravated payment deficits in those developing countries associated with the system. Recent economic activity in the center contributed to the worsening of chronic external imbalances suffered by the majority of developing economies. The increase in oil prices aggravated the situation in a few cases, but this accounted for only 20 percent of the increase in the external deficit of these countries in the last few years. Links between the trilateral system and some of the peripheral countries have also recently taken place.

Despite all this, it must be repeated that the periphery is only marginal to the interests of the trilateral system. This does not mean that the periphery is not aiming to maintain considerable importance within the framework of these interests. It suffices to recall the oil reserves, the size of direct private investment, and the assets of some developing countries. However, the periphery now plays a much less important role in the development of industrial nations than it did during the expansive phase of the world market from the middle of the 19th century. The periphery of the trilateral system encompasses such a multiplicity of situations that it is only in the broadest sense that one can group countries so diverse in size, development, and international importance under the same heading. This divergence, added to the marginal positions held by these countries within the world system, does not lessen the significance of the Third World in contemporary international relations. In the last few years events have taken place within the Third World which had strong repercussions in the center, particularly when they affected relations between the superpowers. When the balance of power between the United States and the Soviet Union is involved, political and military conflicts within the Third World have severe repercussions on international relations. One has only to consider the relation between the Vietnam War and present day tensions in Africa and the Middle East. Also, in the economic field, events occurred which had noticeable effects on the trilateral system. The most significant among them is the OPEC members' increase in the price of oil. The increasing nationalization of basic resources, as well as new policies on foreign investment and on the transfer of technology, have also contributed to upheavals in the traditional relations between the trilateral system and the Third World.

The rapid increase in the private financing of disequilibria in Brazil, Mexico, and other developing countries has lead to a considerable degree of commitment to these countries on the part of the world's financial centers. The links of these financial institutions with the periphery are far from marginal within the context of their worldwide operations. However, this type of situation is not new, nor has it reached the importance it had in former periods. Let us recall, for example, the vast credit given to Argentina by the London Stock Market toward the end of the 19th century, and how the crisis in that country rocked the main financial markets of the time.

In recent years other events have contributed to the increased significance of the periphery to the development of the trilateral system and its links with the rest of the world. On the one hand, there is an inevitable contact among all national and continental entities through the progress of technology, particularly in the fields of transport and communication. Nowadays, any local conflict has international repercussions. On the other hand, there is a growing awareness of the universality of the problems of mankind, and of the inexorable links among peoples and countries. The global studies undertaken on mankind's destiny under the auspices of the Club of Rome, the United Nations, the Bariloche Foundation, and other institutions, have helped to bring to light the planetary dimensions of man's destiny and of international relations. Speculations on the likely depletion of exhaustible resources, the population explosion of the periphery, and environmental pollution have all helped, despite possible exaggerations, to call attention to the universality and inflexibility of current problems.

Within this new context, the group of diverse countries called the Third World has caused a series of important international upheavals. The strong protests of the developing nations within the United Nations and other fora concerning the inequality of present relations in the international order has brought about the need for important revaluations. The New International Economic Order, the Charter of Economic Rights and Duties of States, the conferences of UNCTAD, and the proposals of the Group of Non-Aligned Nations and of the Group of 77, are the most important examples of the revaluation of links between the trilateral system and developing countries. Despite the diversity, disjointedness, and even occasional conflicts of interests within the Third World, its member nations have worked with considerable cohesion in international fora. Certainly, these activities have been rather formal and declarative as opposed to having any real impact on the behavior of the developed countries. But Third World claims have helped create a fluid situation in international relations and have generated a widespread conviction that things cannot go on as they are now. The global dimensions of international relations and of each national experience are causing changes which will have a deep effect on the world system. Such factors as the energy crisis; the link between underdevelopment in the periphery and the dominant factors in the world market; the protection of the world environment; the depth of the political crisis in the industrial countries; and the transfer of Third World conflicts into the world system, all contribute to the general acceptance of the fact that a change in international relations is both necessary and inevitable.

These factors will no doubt acquire growing importance in international relations before too long. But in the foreseeable future one cannot hope for any fundamental changes in the behavior of the trilateral system concerning the periphery. The Conference on International Economic Cooperation, which ended in Paris at the beginning of 1977, revealed the three, present-day limits of the North-South dialogue. First, there is the marginality of the periphery within the central interests of the trilateral system. Second, there is the internal nature of the problems of underdevelopment of most Third World countries and the responsibility of each of them to overcome these problems. Third, there is the fact that a change in the periphery's relations with the trilateral system depends primarily on the ability of developing nations to make unilateral decisions that are sufficiently viable and rational.

The problems of underdevelopment cannot be resolved within the framework of a North-South dialogue, nor can the Third World expect the trilateral system to make decisions which are primarily their own responsibility. Developing countries can expect positive responses from the trilateral system only to decisions taken by themselves. The diffusion of economic power into many large centers, and the existence of still other centers within the socialist group, gives the Third World countries a free hand in the management of their own international relations, a freedom unknown until recently. The predominantly internal nature of the problems of underdevelopment, the fact that the international order allows for new independent policies, and the growing complexity and depth of international relations, create a paradoxical situation. Third World countries are more and more tied to the international order, while at the same time their own decisions are crucial to their domestic transformations and to the revision of their international relations.

Today, the industrial countries' decisions in resolving their own problems of inflation and unemployment are more important to them than cooperation with developing economies. Cooperation measures, as experience shows, have a limited and insubstantial reach and, for reasons stated above, one cannot expect fundamental changes in the autonomous response of the trilateral system to the Third World. High growth rates in the center, overcoming unemployment, and controlling inflation are necessary conditions for the expansion of international trade, the liberalization of access to new products from the periphery for the trilateral markets, and increases in the transfer of financial and technical resources. One cannot but expect that these problems will absorb the bulk of the industrial countries' attention for the time being.

The evolution of relations between the developed and underdeveloped worlds will also be influenced by relations between the superpowers. In the postwar experience, conflicts in the Third World have frequently developed into confrontations between the United States and the Soviet Union. However, for two reasons, the incorporation of conflicts of the underdeveloped world into the field of superpower relations is, to a certain extent, a historical anomaly. First, for the Soviet Union as well as the United States, the periphery does not imperil any vital interests; we have already shown the progressive marginalization of the periphery in international affairs. (On the other hand, the problems of underdevelopment are so great that any attempted interference by the superpowers in the internal affairs of the periphery would cause impossible difficulties, as illustrated in the experiences of the United States in Vietnam and the Soviet Union in Egypt.) Second, to the extent that the superpowers are facing increasing demands for change from within their own societies, they must extend their reciprocal relations, reduce military expenditure, and consequently maintain a more neutral positive vis-a-vis Third World conflicts.

The "neutralization" of Third World sociopolitical tensions in the context of relations between the superpowers may play a positive role in the formulation of a more constructive response by the international community to problems of underdevelopment. Still, for the majority of the developing world, the solution to its problems is in its own hands. The differing capacities for solving these problems among the various countries of the Third World lead one to think that today's differences between these countries will become even more sharp. The designation 'Third World' will become, in the context of international relations, an increasingly less accurate expression.

Aldo Ferrer
Buenos Aires

We wish to start with some definitions and fundamental assumptions.

First, "international order" is to be understood here as the way in which countries have imposed their hegemony by means of their most important social actors (e.g., transnational corporations, power groups, and ruling social classes). That is, "order" refers to the current status quo of world power.

Second, the present international order is considered to be the concrete manifestation of the convergence of power, as expressed through institutions and rules of the international system that have been in force since World War II. This order, which corresponds to a phase that was clearly differentiated from the postwar worldwide capitalist system, began to show the effects of a crisis around 1970.

Third, we assume that economic factors, which are certainly of a crucial nature, should not be studied on an isolated basis without taking into account their concrete social forms; in other words, their close connection to social classes and groups, national governments, international institutions, or transnational corporations.

Fourth, a distinction will be made between, on the one hand, proposals, and on the other, real change in the international system and in the "order" that rules it. By considering which institutions or actors in the international system have implemented a proposal for the new order, it is possible to roughly determine the possibility of a real change in the international system. In this way some of the mistakes that are made when proposals are confused with real processes may be avoided.

Fifth, it is understood that real change in the international system arises from the tendency to concentrate and accrue capital, and from the tensions and contradictions inherent in the postwar international order of 1945-70. These include tensions between the center and the periphery; widening gaps of marginalization and unemployment; and problems arising from expansion and diversification in the socialist world. The dynamics resulting from these complex dialectical processes may make it possible to produce a transition from the postwar order to a new international order.

Lastly, it should be made perfectly clear what is to be understood as the New International Economic Order. The NIEO refers to change called for by Third World countries via their nuclear groups (Group of 77, Non-Aligned Countries, OPEC, etc.) in the fora of the United Nations or outside of them, which have gradually taken shape over the last decades. These proposals show a marked difference from those offered by central capitalist entities such as the Trilateral Commission, OECD, the United States government, and the European Community.

TWO CONCEPTIONS OF THE NIEO

The difference between the NIEO as proposed by the Third World and the First World countries is very great, and until now no negotiations have offered the Third World the realization it demands for these claims.

The effects of the crisis of the postwar capitalist phase are concretely and severely felt at the economic and political levels in Third World countries. But the very existence of the crisis makes it difficult to forecast the development of the international order since the characteristics that might be acquired in the next phase of capitalism are so indeterminate.

At this point there is no noticeable convergence between the new order envisioned by Third World countries and that which currently exists in the international system. Obstacles to the NIEO emerge from the structure of the existing international order, and from attempts to modify it by dominant groups in an effort to preserve their present power structure. Transnational corporations as principal agents of the international order; the concentration of control of the monetary system and of international financing resources within the central countries, especially the United States; and monopolization of technology and production are the major current obstacles to the possibility of establishing a NIEO more equitable for underdeveloped countries.

THE WORLD ECONOMIC CRISIS

During the late 1960s, the economic imbalances that had accumulated during the previous 25 years became critical. The debate on growing international inequality and the failure of plans for aid and development became greatly accentuated. This debate took on different aspects. Generally speaking, it issued in an increase in the proposals for shared claims and cooperation between the Third World and the developed countries. In more concrete and specific terms, there was a rise in liberation movements and nationalist and socialist tendencies in a number of countries. In response, coercion and negotiation have been combined by those at the center of the system, in an effort to maintain the present international order of domination.

The present order has also been threatened, however, by competition within imperialism itself. Deficits in the United States' balance of payments, together with increased productivity on the part of Europe and Japan, have caused an unstable situation for the hegemony of the dollar as international currency. As of 1968 – and in spite of repeated efforts by the IMF – a phase of severe and frequent international monetary fluctuations began, accompanied by inflationary increases which reflected real economic imbalances. However, it was actually toward the end of 1973 that these imbalances were transformed into a general recession – which goes hand in hand with a rise in inflation – of which the increase in oil prices was not the cause, but rather the trigger. The multiplication of the productive capacity of transnational corporations exceeded the solvent demands of the worldwide market.

The characteristics and depth of this world economic crisis have had continuing effects, and as yet hardly any country has managed to consolidate a sustained recuperation process. This in turn has acquired decisive importance in the negotiation of a new international economic order and in the obstacles that confront such negotiation. The crisis not only affected certain national economic areas; it also seriously upset the chain of financial, commercial, and productive interrelations that make up the framework of the worldwide capitalist economy.

This framework consists of much more than the simple convergence of national economics. The trend toward internationalization of capital, which has been in evidence ever since the postwar period and, on a much more intensive level, since the 1960s, has created a worldwide sphere of accumulation which has come to be dominated by transnational companies and conglomerates. This situation has naturally been established in national areas and, basically, in developed countries. However, it has generated its own specific laws of operation. These corporate laws as applied to international accumulation of capital have frequently come into conflict with the legal, political, and economic systems of both developed and underdeveloped countries. Over the past three decades, they have led to a progressive adjustment of these legal systems to the needs for expansion of transnationalized capital. In the same way, they have progressively altered and broadened the international institutional system (IMF, IBRD, GATT, etc.), which regulates economic relations among the countries based on these necessities.

One of the results of the crisis has been to introduce new contradictions and to accentuate those already in existence between national political-economic systems and the operative laws of international accumulation. In effect, in each national sphere, the social agents that prove to be conducive to transnationalization are not always the same. Also, the degree of hegemony that these agents exercise over the other social sectors that make up the whole of society is different in each case.

As the crisis produces its concrete effects – inflation, recession, unemployment, financial upsets – within national areas, the reaction of the affected social classes tends to confirm the top priority status of these areas. The correlation of social, economic, and political forces is a determining factor in the adoption of policies aimed at confronting the consequences of the crisis in each country. Results of the situation include a generalized tendency toward protectionism; the broadening and preservation of international markets; and the transfer of imbalances to other countries via prices, type of exchange, or interest rates. This process was accompanied by instability and political changes in many countries, above all in the peripheral ones.

Basically, the international order was altered as a result of the development of a contradiction between factors that confront the interests of the different social sectors of each country, and those that result from the unequal degree of development of the productive forces in the countries. The intensification of efforts to transfer internal and external effects of the crisis has, in recent years, taken the form of a rise in speculative activity.

Confronting the crisis in this way resulted in a limitation and division of the world market for international movements of capital and goods. That is, the recuperation of the principal national economies, after the recessive phase, worked as a kind of disintegration of the dominant historical tendency toward transnationalization of the economy. The world market, along with the substance of national markets, expanded, but the available space for large-scale reproduction of capital by transnational corporations contracted. This situation, in turn, contributed to prolonging the crisis and to weakening the bases for recuperation. There was an abundance of capital with no productive future.

From the point of view of the underdeveloped countries, the effects have been very disastrous. On the one hand, they have had to bear the weight of the transfer of the crisis in the deterioration of the terms of trade, in a reduction of markets for the majority of their traditional and manufactured export products, in increasing costs for the servicing of an increasing foreign debt, and other areas. On the other hand, in the majority of the countries the social sectors linked to transnationalized capital and the conglomerates themselves have imposed their hegemony on the state in order to promote circumstantial policies that increase economic concentration, foreign debt, and the impoverishment, whether absolute or relative, of the majority of the population.

At present, the oil-exporting countries do not escape this consideration. After the financial boom they experienced around 1974, their position has become reverted in the past three years: they have seen a deadlock in oil prices, a reduction of exports (not only due to conservationist policies), and an increase in the volume and value of their imports as a result of greater integration into the world market.

The political price of the implantation or persistence of highly repressive governments is frequently added to the social cost of the effects of the crisis and of economic policies. The proceedings for mediation between the state and the civilian population (including political parties, unions, etc.) are eliminated and the authoritarian state establishes a legal status that cannot be questioned, and which subordinates national areas to the need for international accumulation.

Transnational companies frequently appear as the social agents that sustain this reordering of the state and society.

This is the context in which the question of a new international economic order is presently being debated. Nations align themselves in different blocs, based on several factors: the degree of development of their productive forces; their position in the world market or in regional markets; the importance of foreign trade in their economic structure; the availability or unavailability of natural, energy, or food resources; the scope of their contracted debt; and, of course, the ideological and political definition of their governments.

THE LIMITS OF CONSENSUS

There are four basic types of general proposals:

a) to eliminate restrictions on international trade;
b) to stabilize the prices of basic raw materials, fuel, and food;
c) to increase economic and financial aid to the poorest countries; and
d) to disseminate technological progress on an international level.

These proposals are all part of the general philosophy for evolving cooperation and reducing inequality among countries. There does appear to be a general consensus concerning the need for ending the present international economic order and establishing a new one.

However, the consensus ends there. Questions of the cause and nature of the present economic crisis, and proposals for how to solve it, vary greatly among the different national governments and economic and financial groups.

The transnational conglomerates, in particular, strive for a new order that will enable them to integrate the world market within the hegemony of their laws of accumulation. The Trilateral Commission, which includes representatives from political parties and institutions in the United States, Japan, and the countries of the European Economic Community, together with executives and major stockholders from the principal conglomerates with holdings in those countries, is a clear expression of the quest for formulas to overcome the economic and political contradictions that impede the full exercise of such a hegemony.

The Third World countries, in turn, attempt to avoid a future in which they would be mere spectators in a new international division of labor that would further increase the concentration of wealth, the exploitation of labor, and the degradation of the environment and natural resources. However, the possibilities for consensus and joint action are weakened by the dissimilar nature of their governments, their internal correlation of social and political forces, and their roles in the scheme of the world economy. Nevertheless, the importance of the search for proposals and actions that assert the identity of the

Third World and its will to cooperate in the face of domination from the center is crucial. To the extent that there is disunity, national sectors will have that much less capacity for foreseeing and responding to new international conditions that might lead to the maximum redistribution of the benefits of development.

THE LIMITS OF COOPERATION

Little by little, there has been opportunity for intergovernmental negotiations, with the participation of the Third World countries. The latter maintain that the United Nations is the framework within which negotiations should take place concerning the NIEO, since the Third World is better represented there than in other institutions which are dominated by the central countries.

The evolution of the contacts and negotiations at these fora is the best indication of the different positions of the peripheral and central countries regarding the creation of the NIEO. However, even though it may be the United Nations where negotiations are carried out, where divergent interests are confronted and where, in fact, agreements and disagreements are reached, this does not mean that the United Nations is the only agency responsible for setting up negotiations and the discussion of positions. It is clear that, just as Third World countries have come to the NIEO bargaining table impelled by the need to eliminate the obstacles that the present international order has imposed on their development, the developed countries have been spurred there by the emergence of elements that disrupt their own economics, by situations that took place in the periphery (liberation movements, OPEC, etc.), and, finally, by the growing conviction that certain reforms must be introduced into the international system in order to maintain its essential and hitherto profitable characteristics.

Based on the divergent and, more often than not, antagonistic interests represented, it is not surprising that the negotiations have followed a difficult path and that the results, from the standpoint of the expectations held by Third World countries, have been very poor.

There is a first stage of claims by developing countries, which actually stem from proposals made by representatives of Third World popular governments, that do not find any response in the formulations expressed by developed countries. For example, the Programme of Action on the Establishment of a New International Economic Order, and the Charter of Economic Rights and Duties of States, were approved at the Sixth Special Session of the United Nations General Assembly in spite of opposition by the industrialized countries. Only Sweden voted in favor of the Charter; the United States, the Federal Republic of Germany, the United Kingdom, Belgium, Denmark, and Luxembourg voted against; the remaining industrialized countries abstained. Hence, the Sixth Special Session ended in basic disagreement between the industrialized countries and those of the Third World.

From then on, however, the attitude of the industrialized countries softened and became more conciliatory; they expressed willingness to start negotiations. However, this still could not be interpreted as actual recognition by the developed countries of the need for a NIEO, at least not in the terms suggested by the Third World countries – as was revealed in later conferences such as the United Nations General Assembly's Seventh Special Session on Development and International Economic Cooperation in New York and the Conference on International Economic Cooperation in Paris.

At the start of the Seventh Session the industrialized countries were willing to hear and discuss the demands stated by Third World nations. Nevertheless, the Western European countries (nine countries from the Common Market that acted as a block in the negotiations) and Japan formed a block with the United States when the discussions approached certain crucial questions. In the end, basic disagreements persisted among the developed countries and the Group of 77 (which now includes approximately 115 countries) on matters such as the need for an integrated and comprehensive program for commodities and others. The discussions reached a complete deadlock in these matters. Although a final document was approved by consensus, it did not include particular recommendations concerning specific courses of action.

The Conference on International Economic Cooperation held in Paris in 1977, was another of the most important examples of trying to reach agreements between industrialized and Third World countries by means of negotiations. Although the reason for this conference was the energy crisis, government representatives from the southern countries included in their agenda other topics pertinent to the discussion of the NIEO. However, the results in this case were very poor as well and the meeting was finally suspended because no progress could be made toward reaching agreement.

Within the framework of the United Nations, the Third World countries have characterized the prevailing situation as one of imperialist domination in which the developed countries are determined to perpetuate their privileged position by means of economic exploitation to be achieved through unequal exchange and by the appropriation of surpluses. The present problem is not scarcity, because ample productive forces and sufficient technological possibilities exist; it is rather a question of an improper distribution of wealth and inadequate use of resources, which means that a major part of the world population has not emerged from a situation of colonial or neocolonial oppression characterized by racial discrimination, apartheid, and the concentration of economic power in the hands of a few nations. In the international system, the powerful nations have guaranteed raw materials at low prices; they increase the added value by processing the materials and then selling the manufactured products at monopolistic prices.

The developed countries have not put into practice measures for improving the situation of the developing countries, although the latter are affected by world inflation, monetary upsets, recession, economic discrimination, and growing protectionism in the developed countries with its discriminatory controls and obstacles to access to technology.

In view of this situation, the Third World countries have formulated the following general principles and political and economic objectives:

a) elimination of colonialism, neocolonialism, racial discrimination, apartheid, and all forms of outside aggression;
b) reinforcement of national sovereignty and effective control over natural resources and economic activities;
c) radical changes in international economic relations and the establishment of new relations based on equality and justice, to eliminate discriminatory economic structures imposed on Third World countries;
d) transformation of the societies of the developing countries, by helping them to accelerate their economic and social progress and reduce their economic dependence on developed countries. This assumes fundamental changes in the socioeconomic structure of developing countries, which in turn should be supported by changes in their relations with the developed countries.

Even though some statements are more radical than others concerning the identification of the causes of underdevelopment, and with regard to the widening of the development gap, the developed countries have accepted (or at least have not dismissed) negotiation as one of the ways for promoting the establishment of the NIEO.

Concerning strategies to be adopted by the developing countries in order to maximize their bargaining power, there are certain guidelines for action that should be pointed out. In the first place, it has been repeatedly stressed that solidarity among all Third World countries must be maintained in order to build up a unified position and begin an irreversible process of change in international relations. In the second place, it has been stated that active, complete, and equal participation by developing countries is necessary in the formulation and implementation of all decisions.

It has also been demonstrated that an alternate strategy of development would be one based on collective self-reliance, whose essential features would be the mobilization of domestic resources, a better distribution of available resources in order to satisfy the basic needs of the population, a weakening of the links with developed countries, and a strengthening of cooperation among Third World countries in order to end dependence on external influences that might exert political pressure or exploitation by means of commercial activities. Mention has also been made of the fact that the establishment of the NIEO cannot remain, as in the past, free from the normal play of market forces and that it should be the result of a conscious policy that has been worked out by the entire international community at large.

From the beginning, the developed countries have openly shown a negative attitude about the establishment of a new world order that would make profound transformations in the present system of international relations. Even when they have agreed to "discussion," they have still expressed strong resistance to initiating new discussions in many key areas. In practice, they maintain an intolerant attitude that reveals a total lack of political will for contributing to the solution of the problems faced by Third World countries.

The governments of the developed countries have not, in fact, prepared any alternative projects with specific proposals. Their proposals are derived from the positions they have adopted when confronted with the demands of the developing countries.

Generally speaking, the developed countries have upheld a position in defense of the status quo, by attempting to impose the idea that the present order of things is beneficial for all, both rich and poor, and that, with a few circumstantial changes or adjustments, the problems that burden the underdeveloped countries can be solved. They have tried to give validity to the thesis that the free play of market forces is the best method for allocating resources and that, as a result, no action should be undertaken which attempts to alter the free market's operation by interfering with supply and demand, nor should any measure be adopted that seeks to substitute alternatives to the market mechanisms.

The fact that, in practice, there is no perfect, open, and free market, and that the way in which the market currently functions seems to have benefited only the developed countries, does not in any way change their line of reasoning, which can be attributed only to the need to defend their interests at all costs, as the present international system does not only in the economic sphere, but in the military and political spheres as well.

The results of negotiations, especially of the Conference on International Economic Cooperation in Paris, demonstrated the following facts:

1. The developed countries proposed concepts diametrically opposed to what an international economic system should be, and to the characteristics the market should have. While Third World countries have fostered a series of regulations in order to protect their position regarding exporting raw materials to the developed countries, the latter have maintained an unconditional stance in defending the "free" market, and have not acknowledged the existence of such essential factors as monopolies, transnationals, and the different countries' unequal bargaining power. On the other hand, insofar as exports of manufactured products from Third World countries are concerned, the developed countries have increasingly established limits, quotas, and tariffs, thereby confirming that they utilize the "market" principles arbitrarily, in accordance with their own interests.

2. The developed countries are not willing to contribute to a total solution of any structural problem. On the contrary, in this regard they have taken up an intransigent position in defense of the status quo.

3. The developed countries do not wish to lose control over the process of promoting the self-reliance and progressive independence of Third World countries. This is especially true in the monetary and financial fields where they have tried to maintain a traditional concept of "aid" within the classic relationship of donor and receiving country.

This has been accentuated by the fact that in most cases this "aid" takes the form of loans, and not of donations or subsidies, as one would be led to believe. Another indication is the indisputable control that the developed countries have over international financial organizations. This power structure would not be altered in the least by the proposals submitted by the developed countries at NIEO negotiations.

4. The topics posed by developing countries are not a main concern for developed countries, whose point of interest centers around matters such as access to raw materials, how to guarantee an appropriate context for foreign investment, and facilitating the operations of transnational corporations.

What is the reason for such negative attitudes? First, there is the permanent need for the expansion of capitalism, which is a process that is inherent in this production system and which demands guaranteeing the control of raw material sources under the terms required by the worldwide accumulation process. Second, there is the need for a certain fluidity in the circulation of financial surpluses in order to guarantee the process of the concentration of capital.

THE ROLE OF TRANSNATIONALS

At another level, however, there appears to be a greater willingness in the developed world to consider NIEO issues, essentially on the part of transnational corporations. This willingness focuses on the acceleration and diversification of economic growth in developing countries, as regards the benefits that the development of different cooperation mechanisms would provide by fulfilling this objective. Hence the developed countries seem to accept the commitment to increase their contribution for promoting and financing multinational projects through which different forms of integration in the agricultural, industrial, and service areas would develop in the Third World.(1) In broad terms, they have abstained from activities that block reaching levels of greater economic integration in these projects.

However, if this situation is viewed from a more correct angle, that is, insofar as it is based on the interests of capitalist development, the promotion of integration projects reveals its true motive, which is the eradication of the impediments to expanding reproduction of capital on a worldwide scale. The projects thereby reproduce and worsen the conditions of exploitation and appropriation that are predominant in international relations. Therefore, an analysis must be made that is not based on a supposed benefit per se from the projects for Third World countries. The concept of collective self-reliance is also a field of battle among the popular sectors and the ruling classes of world capitalism. For the latter, this concept is seen as a simple technical problem of a lack of cooperation mechanisms which can be solved by the creation of appropriate institutional agencies; for the Third World nations it appears as a political tool in the fight for their national and social freedom.

Two closely linked questions must be considered. One is that of the possible solutions for the world capitalist crisis and of the operational methods that have come into play; the other is that of the economic and social convergence that is behind these tendencies and whose structure becomes a requirement for the definitive implantation of new capitalist structures. The first question calls for a model of capitalist accumulation on a worldwide scale, and the second, for a model at the level of the reproduction process of the classes. When they are considered together, they explain the reproduction of capital as a social relationship.

In the first place, we should consider the objective tendency of capital toward internationalization, a tendency of which the growth of transnational corporations is an effect and not a cause. The conglomerate is the necessary form of organization of capital in its present state of concentration and centralization. This point is important in order to understand the role of transnationals in the periphery, and to qualify the kind of actions that should be taken concerning them. On an international level, it is no longer the capital-manufactured goods cycle, which was the predominant system in the first phase of capitalist development, that is carried out. Nor can a complete perspective be attained only by considering the internationalization of the capital-money cycle (a dominant aspect of capitalist expansion ever since the development of the imperialist phase, which established the bases for the predominance of financial capital on a worldwide scale). The cycle of productive capital is now becoming increasingly internationalized. In this process, national territories are no longer the central area of production, which becomes integrated and planned within a new productive unit: the transnational corporation. This is placed above and beyond national borders, although it maintains its decision making center in the countries, thereby maximizing the profit gains of the whole group and not necessarily of any one of its affiliates. Hence transnationals become the principal agents of a process which at this stage constitutes an antimony between economics and politics. This is a contradiction of capitalism: the potential development of open levels of conflict between transnationals and their countries of origin.(2)

At another level, this process means the maximum development of capital as a social relationship, and the tendency toward the exclusivism of capitalist production on a worldwide scale. The basic condition has been the development of a world labor market of potential use to transnational corporations.

The analysis of the industrialization processes in the developing countries should be made within this general framework. However, and this is particularly relevant for Latin American countries, the new tendencies have modified some of the conditions for industrialization. The integration of production on a worldwide scale within the framework of accumulation of transnational corporations results in a unique and integrated market. In fact, the tendencies of the world economy determine the direction of industrialization at the periphery, orienting it mainly toward the world market. In this sense, the relocation of industrial activities — the industrial "redeployment" that transfers productive processes to the periphery — appears possible, although it is unstable as yet within the context of the current crisis.

This method for the integration of the periphery adds large contingents of labor to the capital reproduction process without offering a parallel solution to the unemployment problems of these countries. In this way conditions are created that make it possible to substantially raise the rate of profit and to partially solve the valorization problems presently faced by capitalism. This is the prime mover in the expansionist method: the possibility of taking full advantage of the low salaries paid in the peripheral countries, which are a product of the historical development of their integration in the capitalist world economy. On the other hand, the effective implantation of the model requires that this condition absolutely be maintained. This leads us to the matter of the social convergence that is derived from the new tendencies.

The internationalization process led by transnationals is formed in association with local dominant sectors that benefit from monopolization and from participation in integration plans. In this way, the demarcation line between imperialist capital and national capital, insofar as they are bearers of opposing bourgeois projects, progressively fades in order to leave the way open to a homogenization of the interests of monopolistic capital, which in turn leads to domination-subordination relationships with other less developed and less important bourgeois sectors. On the other hand, the middle layers, affected by the weakening of their economic base, find their political power reduced, while the exclusive nature of the model and the acute contradictions it fosters find a correlate in the authoritarian and repressive political systems that usually accompany it.

In the case of the developed countries, these general guidelines also lead to the imposition of new conflicts on existing contradictions. On the one hand redeployment, which tends to obey the logic of capital expansion and is therefore handled at this stage by transnationals, implies unemployment and lowered salaries.(3) On the other hand, redeployment also implies a weakening of the ability of less efficient proprietary sectors to take advantage of new markets and locations. Hence the quest for formulas by developed nations to avoid the destabilizing pressures of the new guidelines is a short-term tendency. Eventually, it is possible that transnationals will increase their pressure for a reordering of states based on their possibilities for expansion, which would lead to greater severity in the domestic political processes as a response to worsening social conflicts.

If this tendency should become a reality, it would mean a greater concentration of income on a worldwide scale, determined by the guidelines for the appropriation of surpluses generated within the system as a whole, and ruled by bourgeois sectors that have been transnationalized beyond their own particular origins. Increasing pressure will be exerted on the popular sectors, and this will tend to increase the inequality of the stratification by giving privileges to a smaller and more highly skilled class. This is how the integration methods fostered by transnationals actually affect possibilities for broader cooperation based on the self-determination and self-interest of Third World majorities.

CONCLUSIONS

The obstacles to a more just new order may be summarized in the following points:

1. The manner in which the imperialist division of labor is being restructured makes it possible to foresee, in the periphery, the emergence of new industrial processes which will be a top priority in the world market.

2. The vast development of the technology that made possible, on the one hand, multiple fragmentation of the productive process and, on the other, the utilization of unskilled labor, will favor industrial transfer to the periphery and its partial localization in different countries, based on available natural resources and the given conditions in the labor market.

3. The development of productive integration processes and the adoption of different trade cooperation mechanisms are possible means of overcoming the obstacles to the new order. However, as these processes come into contact with local bourgeoisies and expanding transnational corporations, their development will gradually be subsumed under prevailing exploitation-subordination relationships.

4. The cooperation mechanisms will not result in greater independence for the Third World; on the contrary, they will mean greater solidarity for the ruling classes on a worldwide scale. Nor will these mechanisms provide an income redistribution favoring the impoverished masses; rather, their rationale resides in the increased exploitation of labor.

5. If the new model is implanted and redeployment represents an alternative for overcoming the crisis of capital, competition may develop among the ruling classes of the periphery, since they stand to profit as receivers of the transfer of surpluses. In any event, greater economic capacity will result from successfully guaranteeing the political stability needed for diminishing investment risks and keeping domestic salaries low.

These obstacles to cooperation are not unsolvable. In the first place, redeployment is hindered by the persistence of protectionist measures that originate in the disintegration process of the world market. If channels for exports in the periphery, whose domestic market for new production is limited, are not opened up, redeployment is no longer attractive. In addition, the social and political contradictions that this strategy exacerbates are generating wide breaches in the power blocs of many developing countries, especially in Latin America. Parallel to this, the redemocratization proposals that accompany these political crises open the way to a greater capacity for the mobilization of the popular sectors.

Future prospects for Third World countries are based on the contradictory developments of growing transnationalization and the affirmation of sovereignty and cooperation. Collective self-determination will be a renovating concept in international relations if it affirms the redistribution of power in developing societies, so that existing structures are progressively altered and exploitative relations are eliminated. Hence, a new domestic order is both a requirement and a constitutive part of a truly new international order.

Enrique Oteiza
Jorge Fontanals
Fernando Porta
Susana Schkolnik
Caracas

NOTES

(1) Constantino V. Vaitson, Crisis en la Cooperacion Economica Regional: La integracion entre paises subdesarrollados (Mexico: ILET, 1978).

(2) Immannuel Wallerstein, "An Historical Perspective on the Emergence of the N/O," mimeo, (Caracas: CENDES, 1977).

(3) See Pedro Vuskovic, "La restructuracion del capitalismo mundial," Commercio Exterior 28, no. 3 (March 1978).

II

Prospects and Problems of the New International Economic Order

3 A Diagnosis of Failures and Prospects

Miguel S. Wionczek,
Mexico

THE CURRENT STATE OF NIEO NEGOTIATIONS: DEADLOCK

At the end of the 1970s, years after the North-South dialogue was launched at the United Nations, the dialogue has reached an almost complete stalemate on all issues, both major and minor. Considering this worrisome trend, this paper will attempt to shed some light on three broad questions: a) what has gone wrong with the NIEO negotiations; b) what issues underlie the deadlock; and c) is there any way out of the stalemate.

The author assumes that the New International Economic Order is needed not because the traditional order is wicked, immoral, or unjust but because in the longer run it does not bring real benefits to anyone in our rapidly changing international political, social, and economic situation. The best evidence that the present international economic order is inadequate is that it has led the world economy into chaos.

In spite of the voluminous and continuously increasing literature on the subject, the NIEO(1) cannot be defined at all and perhaps, since it is a dynamic set of multiple objectives obtainable only through difficult multilateral negotiations, it should not be defined. As regards the broad areas in which a substantial revision of the traditional rules of the international political and economic game is badly needed, these have been identified in official United Nations documents and elsewhere. They include international trade in raw materials and manufactured goods, international technology trade, international flows of both public and private capital, and the international monetary system.(2) To this impressive list we should add the international control of natural resources which are potentially available, in the seabed and in space, through recent technological advances.

There are by now a considerable number of technically competent schemes and policy proposals in all these fields, which reflect the general philosophy of the NIEO. Most of them have been elaborated not by Third Word "radicals," but by academic experts from the developed

47

countries, acting in their personal capacities or as staff members of international organizations. Many proposals go back to the ideas which circulated in the Western world in the thirties and in the early forties. Some are associated with the name of John Maynard Keynes.   Since, because of the opposition of the advanced Western countries on the one hand, and the frequent lack of consensus among the developing countries on the other, none of the recent NIEO initiatives has reached the stage of implementation, it may be worthwhile to present a full list of the present deadlocked areas.

1. The UNCTAD proposals to establish the Integrated Programme for Commodities, supported by the Common Fund, for the purpose of eliminating extreme price fluctuations of the principal raw materials and foodstuffs and thereby assuring a certain degree of export revenue stability for developing country producers, ran into a seemingly final deadlock at the end of 1978. Despite the fact that in three unsuccessful negotiations during 1977-78 the project's sponsors scaled it down considerably, it is still opposed because of its alleged financial implications.(3)

2. Individual commodity negotiations, which were to cover some 15 products according to the UNCTAD IV agreement reached at Nairobi in 1976, and which were supposed to pave the way toward the Integrated Programme for Commodities, have made practically no progress, and only one commodity agreement (on sugar) has been renegotiated during the two-and-a-half years that followed UNCTAD IV.(4)

3. Multinational trade negotiations under GATT, known as the Tokyo Round, concentrated mostly on non-tariff trade restrictions, and were not completed by the end of 1978 as expected. While the ultimate results of the negotiations will somewhat improve the position of the developing countries in regard to the access of their manufactures for the developed country markets, growing developed country protectionism (particularly in the field of consumer goods, which account for the major part of the developed countries' manufacturing exports) has more than offset the Tokyo Round's achievements.(5) Certainly, the "informal" or "voluntary" export restrictions negotiatied outside GATT would have hit the developing countries even more severely, if it were not for the fact that a large part of their manufactured exports originates in the affiliates of transnational corporations, or in their own firms subcontracted by TNCs to produce parts and/or to assemble final products for exports to the developed countries.(6)

4. The flows of official development assistance from international agencies under bilateral arrangements are declining in real terms and as a percentage of the GNP of the developed countries, not only because of world inflation but also because of the accumulation of the service burden on the outstanding debts of developing countries.(7)

5. Concomitantly with the declining role of official development assistance and the stagnation of the flows of private venture capital to the developing countries, the role of private banking in the development financing of these countries continues to increase; the developing countries' total long-term (over one year) liabilities to international

private banks exceeded, in 1978, those to official multilateral and bilateral financial agencies. Despite the large growth of their external public debt which (including short-term commercial debt) was estimated at the end of 1976 at some $225 billion, no agreement has been reached at UNCTAD or elsewhere on common rules and criteria for possible debt renegotiations. Moreover, notwithstanding the growing number of instances, such renegotiations take place on an ad hoc, case-by-case basis.(8)

6. Debt relief measures for the poorest developing countries, agreed to in early 1978 in the form of transforming official loans into grants, have not been put into practice by some major developed countries, including the United States, presumably because of domestic legislative difficulties.

7. At the World Bank and the IMF the periodic discussions about replenishment of the Bank's resources and the expansion of the Fund's quotas are proceeding at a slower pace than ever in response to domestic financial and monetary considerations and because of the global liquidity excess (the Eurocurrency market, outside the control of national monetary authorities of the major developed countries, has been estimated in early 1978 at over $700 billion).

8. No progress has been made and none is in sight on the subject of linking Special Drawing Rights (SDRs) with development financing.

9. The orderly functioning of the international monetary system under the current flexible exchange rates proves at least as difficult as under the previous fixed rates, as demonstrated by extreme exchange rates fluctuations during 1978. The defense of the U.S. dollar, announced by President Carter on Nov. 1, 1978, and the agreement on the European currency unit (ECU), reached in Brussels one month later by seven out of the nine members of the European Economic Community, did not eliminate acute concerns about the future of the international monetary system.(9)

10. UNCTAD negotiations on the international code of conduct for technology transfer, begun in 1975, reached a deadlock in November 1978 on the key issues of its legality and implementation machinery; the U.N. Negotiating Conference on the Code, convoked in the fall of 1978, looks more and more like another U.N. Conference on the Law of the Sea.(10)

11. The U.N. Conference on the Law of the Sea itself has recently run into a new stalemate after eight consecutive sessions; little progress is in sight.

12. Even relatively minor international agreements, such as the UNCTAD Code of Conduct for Maritime Conferences, adopted in 1975 after several years of negotiations, lack implementation. In this particular case failure to reach the necessary minimum number of ratifying countries has not prevented it from taking effect three years after the date of the final agreement.

13. Finally, notwithstanding the large volume of rhetoric devoted to the concepts of national or regional self-reliance, progress in economic and technological cooperation among the developing countries has been

minimal, although only a dozen of them can envisage some degree of individual, self-reliant development.(11)

Developed Country Resistance

Since the underlying philosophy of the NIEO is essentially reformist and aims at improving the existing mechanism of international relations rather than changing the existing structures, it may be surprising that the implementation of the NIEO meets with so many difficulties on the part of the developed countries – who presumably suscribe to liberal economic norms, and should be interested in a progressive reform of the present set of international economic relations, on account of their growing inadequacy for meeting their own objectives. As was pointed out recently, ". . .a number of the key elements of the NIEO programme have clear stabilizing effects on the existing economic system and, in the long run, their implementation may possibly even give the kiss of death to the pursuit of vigorous restructuring."(12)

Thus, for example, the implementation of the UNCTAD Integrated Programme for Commodities would not affect the longer-term interests of the developed countries (for instance, security of their access to raw materials), but might help greatly in the management of international and domestic business cycles. The increase in the volume of official financial assistance to developing countries would undoubtedly increase the volume of the developed countries' manufactured exports to these countries. More orderly functioning of the international monetary system would not only eliminate undue private speculation against weaker currencies, including the dollar, but would lower the barriers against international flows of capital to the developing countries. The successful negotiation of a code of conduct for international technology transfer would not only set the rules of the game for the only segment of international trade which is presently left completely out of the realm of regulation and surveillance, but, through its contribution to the domestic technological capability of developing countries, it might also help to alleviate serious international tensions arising due to worldwide capitalist and socialist competition. If these interests were to behave more rationally, many obstacles to the revision and modernization of the traditional economic order could be overcome with relative ease. The developed countries defend, however, their short-term national interests, and the advanced socialist countries continue to proclaim their lack of responsibility for the results of the "exploitative excesses of the capitalist system." Since the developing countries are not helpful either, the obstacles to the NIEO appear formidable.

Developing Countries Resistance

The Developing countries fail to be helpful on a number of grounds. First, under the guise of the defense of their individual sovereignty, they were able to divorce the question of international reform from that of a new domestic economic and social order. The fact is, however, that the equity of internal political, social, and economic relations in most developing countries leaves much to be desired, to say the least. Moreover, nobody can explain how the postulated improvement of equity in international relations can translate into more equitable domestic social and economic practice in developing countries in the absence of a commitment of the actual leaders of these countries to social and economic reforms. The dense fog surrounding these uncomfortable issues at the United Nations affects the credibility of the NIEO and puts serious limitations upon the potential support it might receive from the more progressive sectors of public opinion in the developed countries.

Second, the common front of the developing countries in the NIEO negotiations, formed in 1974-75 under the impact of OPEC's success, is now crumbling. While some people claim that the growing conflicts and frictions among the developing countries are the result of political manipulation by developed countries, they are also attributable to two specific but rarely mentioned factors: major differences in the size and development levels of the members of the Group of 77, and the growing impact of the present world economic crisis upon individual developing countries. The emergence of Third World concerns in the final years of the relatively satisfactory albeit unequal postwar performance of the world economy, and the progressive deterioration of world economic conditions in the seventies led many developing countries to embark on the double path of populist policies at home and "third-worldism" at the international level. With the general defeat of populism in Latin America and Southern Asia, and the consequent return to conservative domestic social and economic policies, developing countries support for cooperation on issues of the NIEO at the United Nations and elsewhere was superseded by pragmatic approaches to immediate internal difficulties.(13)

Fragmentation and New Actors

Consequently, given that the advanced countries have always preferred conservative pragmatism and special relations of a bilateral type, individual dialogues between the different parts of the North and the South reappeared on the international scene, eroding the support for the NIEO in most major and middle-size developing countries. The intense flirtation between industrial countries and the so-called newly industrializing countries (Argentina, Brazil, Mexico, India, Algeria, and some export-oriented East Asian countries) offers evidence to this effect. The Japanese interest as a silent partner in the Association of South East Asian Nations (ASEAN), and France's support for the economic reorganization of black Africa, can be understood only within this political framework. It may even be unfair to complain about the disenchantment of the Third World with the long-term NIEO strategy.

In a world in which the Western industrial countries adopt such individualistic, pragmatic attitudes, it may be too much to expect the much weaker developing countries to act otherwise.

Intra-Third World conflicts and frictions, together with the failure of the populist "reforms" and the disenchantment with the lack of progress on the NIEO front, led inevitably to the decline of Third World capacity to negotiate with the advanced countries at the United Nations and elsewhere. As was to be expected, the growing lack of interest in the major industrial capitals in the long-term objectives of the NIEO resulted in the steady deterioration of the political and technical level of developing countries negotiators in international fora. The parallel bureaucratization of international agencies themselves further compounded the difficulties. In brief, the responsibility for the NIEO stalemate does not fall exclusively on the shoulders of heartless neocolonialists.

Additional complications arise from the fact that there are more actors in the NIEO game than is generally assumed. The confrontation and the negotiations involve not only the developed capitalist countries, the Group 77, and the socialist states (including, as a separate actor, China), but two other groups of actors as well: transnational corporations, and the members of the incipient public global system (both the U.N. and the non-U.N. international agencies, and their regional and subregional extensions). These new actors entered the international decision making process in the past 20 years. It would be an error or an oversight to consider them, as some do, a reflection of a new global private conspiracy, or an expression of a new global public power.

While differing functionally from nation-states, both transnational corporations and international public agencies are in many ways similar to them. Much like nation-states, they are of varying size and development level, and are endowed with different degrees of power. Also, like nation-states, these newly emerged actors have four major objectives: survival, security, welfare, and power. While only one of these objectives (welfare) has an explicitly economic content, economic issues play implicit, and at times important roles in the other three areas. Moreover, all categories of actors, old and new, have something else in common – they can function only if and when they consist of hierarchical structures whose members are bound by loyalties to the respective structures.

Transnational corporations

According to conventional radical wisdom, transnational corporations not only represent the last stage of economic imperialism, but they are the tail which wags the dog – the latter being the advanced capitalist state. Moreover, it is assumed that transnationals are not only bent upon the economic exploitation of our planet through the maximization of profits and hence the accumulation of political power, but that they also provide the ideological underpinning and support for capitalist forces fighting against the advance of socialism. Acting allegedly as a kind of joint chiefs of staffs in the antisocialist crusade, transnationals are said to be particularly mischievous in the developing countries by interfering in their economic, financial, social, and political life and forging all sorts of chains that make practically impossible the fulfill-ment of national objectives of either the new or the old developing countries. This line of reasoning represents "scapegoatism" in its purest form, and leads easily to the defeatist but nonetheless comfortable conclusion that the New International Economic Order is simply impos-sible to achieve as long as transnational corporations, and capitalism itself, are not forever banished from the world.

It may be more useful to assume simply that in search of the fulfillment of their own objectives, transnational corporations interfere with all other actors of the international game, and interfere more with weak nation-states than with strong ones. Once one accepts that among the important but sometimes conflicting objectives of TNCs are not only economic power but also survival, security, and the welfare of their "citizens," it becomes easier to understand their otherwise con-fusing international behavior. Thus, since they are deeply interested in survival, they enter willingly into arrangements with the socialist states even though they prohibit external proprietary control of their eco-nomic activities. Similar longer-term security considerations make them accept co-ownership and co-production formulas in many non-socialist states, although these would have been unthinkable only a quarter of a century ago. Finally, welfare (and growth) considerations explain the TNCs' strong and sustained participation in world scientific and technological progress.

On the other hand, conflicts between the objectives of the TNCs and those of other actors on the international scene often cause untold headaches not only to the governments of developing countries but to those of developed countries as well, as demonstrated by the present international monetary problems of the Washington policy makers. Furthermore, the quasi-autonomous behavior of TNCs may lead to the emergence of new international coalitions, as in the case of OPEC. It is difficult to say, for example, whether OPEC's life and future depends more on the cooperation of the TNCs in distributing their oil wordwide, than the fate of the "seven sisters" and large oil "independents" depends on OPEC. New coalitions are arising through common export interests between TNCs and newly industrializing countries in which they oper-ate, and between TNCs and countries in a position to think about expanding manufactured exports to developed industrial markets. As a matter of fact, in a world of growing protectionist pressures, TNCs may represent one of the few allies available to some developing countries in the field of international trade.

Given their strong position in the world economy, TNC relations to the NIEO cannot be reduced, as many believe, to one single item of the long NIEO agenda – a code of conduct for transnational corporations. Whether one likes it or not, the presence of TNCs affects most of the NIEO agenda. Consequently, little progress will be made on that whole front unless some new modus vivendi is arrived at through negotiations between the proponents of the NIEO and this set of private inter-national actors. Unfortunately, present developments in the developing countries are not particularly conducive to such a new modus vivendi, since the latter would call for an increase in Third World bargaining power. Overpowered by an apocalyptic vision of the strength and the inflexibility of TNCs, and disenchanted with the NIEO, many developing countries have been recently surrendering whatever new bilateral economic relationships they were able to establish with TNCs in the past decade.

International public agencies

This brief survey of the NIEO actors would not be complete without an overview of international public agencies which center on, but do not limit their range of action to, the U.N. system. The U.N. itself has undergone very considerable evolution since its establishment in San Francisco in 1945 by 50 signatories of its charter. Contrary to the belief of some idealistic souls, the U.N. is not the expression of a new global power, nor a world government in its initial stage. Composed of the secretariat, a dozen specialized, semi-autonomous (and in the financial field even totally autonomous) agencies, regional commissions, and other permanent or ad hoc bodies and expert groups, it reflects the spontaneous and at times chaotic expansion of the agenda of inter-national relations.

In spite of having faced a permanent financial crisis for the past 20 years and having been burdened by a sizable external debt, the U.N. manages somehow not only to survive but to marshal and manage increasing financial and human resources. It gives employment to many thousands of people stationed all over the world. It establishes highly hierarchical structures and expects from its personnel a kind of basic loyalty of "international civil servants." Its strength comes not only from its global ideology but from its growing bureaucracy.

The U.N. system started as a mainly political body dominated by the West, particularly the United States, and progressively became an open-ended and permanent "global assembly" for the treatment of almost any subject under the sun. The interests of its 151 member states are represented not only by permanent diplomatic missions in New York, Geneva, and elsewhere, but also by different national groups in the secretariats of the system. These secretariats are described by critics as a bureaucratic hydra, or as a sort of medieval monarchy, or as a very special kind of inefficient transnational public corporation. Whatever its shortcomings, and whatever the similarities of its behavior to that of other actors on the international scene, the successive failures of attempts to change the U.N. organization during the past 15 years strongly suggest that the U.N. is not only unique, but is the best available organization in the international public realm.

Unfortunately, the system's productivity, efficiency, and impact upon world affairs, which have never been optimal, are declining. Moreover, its shortcomings seriously affect the prospects for the NIEO.

Most of these shortcomings are directly related to the U.N. system's main objectives, which are basically the same as those of other internationally active social groups: survival, security, welfare, and power. Other impediments arise from the fact that not only do the people who man the systems often have divided loyalties and specific individual interests, but in some instances the international civil service itself is still an ideal rather than a full-fledged reality.

The U.N. system, at the center and in its affiliates, branches, agencies, and dependencies as well (using the language of transnationals and empires), is run in the broadest terms by three categories of people: globally thinking moralists, skillful political operators, and non-imaginative bureaucrats. Over time, the numerical participation of operators and bureaucrats has disproportionately increased, partly in response to the dynamics of the system itself, and partly because of the expansion of its geographical scope of influence and the way it recruits its personnel. These trends have been strengthened by the fact that the system offers a refuge – in political, financial, and individual security terms – to people who might have a tough life outside of the realm of international public bureaucracy. All these factors are at the heart of what is known to many inside and outside observers as the crisis of the U.N.

This crisis reflects not only the behavior of nation-states but the system's internal problems. The following affect particularly the system's ability to deliver international services of mediation and conflict resolution:

a) the detachment of the "global policy strategists" from real life, which is very reminiscent of the attitudes of global military planners in the military establishments of major national powers;
b) the concomitant tendency to consider verbal expressions of partial negotiated agreements "in principle" (declarations, resolutions, and reports) as the equivalent of action;
c) the interpretation of such "action" through the particular spectacles of conflicting short-run interests of individual agencies and units, which results in the unending process of intrasystem bureaucratic negotiations and affects severely the quality and the relevance of substantive work, including studies, reports, and policy-oriented initiatives (the overburdening of the international public system with these intra-negotiations under the guise of coordination among different units resulted in the shift of the substantive work almost exclusively to ad hoc expert committees and outside consultants);
d) the substitution of innovative actions by repetitive exercises along the lines of fashionable global subjects; and
e) the extremely low weight ascribed to the implementation of agreed decisions under the pretext that the implementation is a matter to be dealt with exclusively at the national level.

These principal shortcomings and limitations of the international public system affect the actual negotiations of the NIEO as much as the conflicts of interest among nation-states and their groupings, and the global activities of transnational corporations. In spite of the volume of work done over the past years on the subject of the reorganization of the U.N. system, its shortcomings have not been studied in sufficient detail. Moreover, it is both curious and symptomatic that the NIEO proponents dedicate very little attention to them.   Instead, they concentrate on such issues as the representation of different countries and regions in the secretariats of international public agencies, and the voting formulas in the agencies themselves.   Thus, for example, in many places it is hopefully assumed that if only more people from the LDCs were working in international public agencies, and if the voting rules in such bodies as the World Bank and the IMF were adjusted to new political realities, the international system would improve its performance in favor of LDCs, and consequently the NIEO would progress at a more rapid pace. There is no evidence available as yet that would lend support to these general propositions, which may be considered as the necessary but by no means sufficient conditions for the progress of the NIEO. One would wish that conferences on the NIEO would dedicate more attention to the decision making processes at the U.N. and the non-U.N. international public agencies.   Most writers presumably assume that the function of the international public system is to hold meetings, to pass resolutions, and to publish reports. Afterwards, God will take care of the NIEO. An alternative diagnosis suggests that "the NIEO is impeded by institutional proliferation and the lack of a coherent and coordinated approach to the economic and social agenda at both international and national levels, and by the failure of the international secretariat to inspire confidence and analyze progress."(14)

In summary, the fact that in real life there is a considerable degree both of overlap and conflict between objectives, structures, and loyalties of the three major categories of actors at the international level – nation-states, transnational corporations, and international agencies – greatly complicates the decision making process in respect to the NIEO. Only against the background of the maze of relations among multiple categories of international actors, with their individual and group objectives and particular loyalties, can the difficulty of creating the New International Economic Order be understood. If the task were limited to the interaction of nation-states only, perhaps it would be easier to achieve. The relatively smooth working of the international system between the Napoleonic wars and 1914 offers circumstantial but not convincing evidence in that respect.(15) It should be remembered, however, that in the 19th century there were less than 10 nation-states that really mattered, and the total of independent or quasi-independent national entities did not exceed 40.

A CRISIS OF REALISM

Thus, in social and economic matters both international and national, the world is doing much worse than at any time since the early thirties, though not so much in terms of absolute performance as in relation to expectations. In the developed market-oriented Western societies, a quarter century of rapid postwar material progress resulted in the general acceptance of full employment, job security, and high-level individual consumption as unquestionable social and individual goals to be regarded as part and parcel of basic human rights. In the industrialized socialist societies, which in terms of individual consumption are less than 20 years behind the Western capitalist world, and which provide their members with employment and job security as a matter of course, current expectations are putting increasing emphasis on the weakest part of the package – individual consumption and individual political rights. In the underdeveloped periphery, the demonstration effect of the two different packages of social and individual welfare available in the advanced world result in a highly idealized vision of the optimal society. This vision is a composite version of the most attractive elements of the capitalist and of the socialist worlds. It comprises as instant objectives full employment, job security, high-level consumption, and individual freedoms.

This idealized vision conveniently forgets, first, that it took the capitalist West some 200 years to arrive at its present stage of technology-based prosperity, and second, that it took the USSR, the centerpiece of the socialist system, over half a century to leave behind the state of general backwardness – which, we should add, could at no time have been compared with the underdevelopment characteristic today of most of the periphery, particularly in ex-colonial Africa and Asia. The idealized vision of the "best of all worlds" also conveniently forgets the historically high social cost of building modern capitalism in the West and socialist welfare states in Eastern Europe. Only serious social and economic scholars of the history of Western Europe between 1789 and 1870, of the United States between the civil war and 1914, and of the Soviet Union between 1917 and 1953, are aware of these uncomfortable "details."

Considering, on the one hand, the challenge offered by the overall level of welfare achieved in the advanced capitalist and socialist countries as well as the degree of recent scientific and technological progress, and, on the other hand, by the general level of poverty, hunger, and unemployment, the concurrent lack of basic political rights, and the rising level of minimal expectations in most of the developing countries, the present world performance is quite disappointing. Notwithstanding the rhetoric of interdependence and international cooperation, the objectives of survival, security, welfare, and power are fostered by traditional means and unilateral policies whether nationally, or by international public agencies and transnational corporations. The failures at national or – keeping in mind the actual shrinking of the world – tribal level are particularly striking. The frustrations of national social and economic policies both in the developed nations and the developing countries constitute a general global crisis.

While academics and some politicians in the advanced North talk about the necessity of substituting for the concept of growth that of development, and increasing claims are heard about the urgent need to "do something" about global basic needs, short-term policies in the developed countries fail to assure the growth even of the North itself. A passive consensus seems to be emerging both in capitalist and socialist countries to the effect that the continuation of the economic growth rates of the past 25 years is no longer possible.(16)

Much of time, money, and human energy are dedicated to rationalizing a triple thesis that rapid economic growth is neither possible, feasible, nor advisable, since the basic human needs of the advanced societies have been (almost) fulfilled, and there are physical (resource) limits to growth. On the other hand those in the developed countries who have lately embraced the concern about basic needs in the underdeveloped peripheries, and who suggest that they return to agricultural pursuits and to "small is beautiful" types of technologies as a defense against the excesses of industrial civilization, seem not to notice the increasing idleness of the existing productive facilities in the advanced countries, and keep silent about the misuse of a large part of these facilities for purposes completely divorced from the peaceful application of capital, labor, and natural resources for development. Many spokesmen for the developing countries and the NIEO skirt the same issues when related to the developments in their own sphere of influence.

In brief, we are facing the progressively static framework of decelerating growth, worldwide inflation, open and disguised unemployment, growing indebtedness, monetary crisis, growing social tensions, and the progressive bureaucratization of societies and international structures. The only activity which seems to prosper is the search for national security and power through the arms race.(17) One should not be surprised, the world being what it is, to find that the arms race is contagious. Those same developing countries which clamor for the new economic order based upon better international morality and equity, do their utmost to reallocate power to themselves by means of increasing their own military capabilities. The elimination of military dependence through the establishment of local military industries, and, whenever possible, of the nuclear strike capability, is quite fashionable in many major developing countries these days.(18)

The NIEO has as its supreme objective the harmonization of interests at national and international levels between the developed and the underdeveloped parts of the world economy. This objective is to be achieved through negotiations within a dynamic context of economic growth, social development, scientific and technological progress, and political accommodation. Unfortunately, however, not only are the forces of dynamic economic growth missing in the capitalist West and in the underdeveloped South, and perceptibly weakening in the socialist East, but it becomes more and more difficult to discern the dynamic factors of scientific and technological progress both on the global and on the national scale.

With the growth rates in the Western developed countries declining steadily and those in the socialist and the underdeveloped countries sustained to some extent through external borrowing for consumption against the future,(19) an increasing worldwide concern can be detected(20) about the steady decline of the accumulation rate of scientific discovery and technological innovation. In reaction to such trends, and in light of the uncertain future of the world economy as well as each major country's necessity to defend its share in world trade, many people envision the emergence of technological protection measures, a corollary of the increasing wave of trade protectionism. In the highly industrialized economies the slowdown in the application of new science and technology for the production of goods and services and for the increase of welfare is explained by the trap of the vicious circle of slow growth – the fall in investment followed by the fall in the application of science and technology for development. In the socialist countries, which seem to depend to an increasing degree on Western technology, the responsibility is shifted to bureaucratic over-centralization. Finally, in the developing countries, because of local social and cultural constraints as well as inadequate types and channels of technology transfer from the advanced Western countries, science and technology can hardly prosper anyway.

Consequently the weakness of the contributions of science and technology to the needs of the developing countries compounds world-wide social tensions, deriving from antiquated political and economic structures, acute welfare differences between the advanced industrial centers and the backward peripheries, and increasing welfare gaps within the underdeveloped societies themselves. Since international and national conditions conducive to NIEO negotiations within the framework of a positive non-zero sum game are largely absent, the political accommodation of conflicting interests becomes extremely difficult, if not impossible.

PREREQUISITES OF PROGRESS

Some people consider that the North-South economic issues are the key global problems faced by the world during the rest of the late 20th century. We attempted to demonstrate, however, that this particular set of problems has been accompanied and complicated by other, not less important global issues: military and security problems between East and West, exacerbated by the trend toward military independence in the South and by nuclear proliferation; North-South political problems due to the rise of nationalism; conflicts between TNCs and nation-states centered around the issue of control and distribution of profits from productive, mainly industrial, activities; and problems arising in the international public system (including the United Nations) with respect to the sovereignty of the nation-states.

Any strategy for the NIEO must take into account the links between all these global issues. In other words, in addition to the explicit interdependence between problems of trade, development finance, technology, and the international monetary system, which form the NIEO agenda, there is an implicit interdependence between military and political issues on the one hand, and social and economic conflicts on the other, on global, regional, and bilateral levels. Acknowledging these two types of interdependence does not necessarily imply that all issues can be negotiated in a single package. The failure of the Paris Conference (CIEC) has demonstrated that even the negotiation of the NIEO package itself is very difficult.

A clear vision of the interdependence of all major global issues is needed to get the NIEO out of its present stalemate, responsibility for which rests with the lack of political will on the part of the advanced Western countries, with serious internal short-run difficulties of the developing countries, and with the inefficiency of the international bureaucracy. The stalemate is also the result of the absence at the negotiating table of two other groups of actors: the socialist states which account for about one-third of the world population, and the transnational enterprises which represent about one-half of inter-national trade.

Socialist Country Participation

The absence of the socialist states from the NIEO debates and the CIEC in Paris, and their passive participation elsewhere, are contrary to their own long-term interests. It is one thing to deny all responsibility for the past; it is another not to participate — or to be excluded from — the process of negotiating the shape of changes in the future. Moreover the actual and potential breakdowns of the existing political and economic order (postwar developments in South East Asia, the crisis in Iran) are pregnant with dangers for everybody, including the socialist countries. Nature abhors a vacuum, and chaotic regional or local situations can easily spill over into confrontations among nuclear superpowers. Thus, one of the major prerequisites for any progress on the NIEO front is the permanent presence and the active participation of the socialist seg-ment of the world economy.

TNC Participation

The complaint about the absence of TNCs from negotiations on the NIEO may sound almost treasonable to the NIEO's proponents. It is of little help, however, to deal with any of the major parties to the dispute through intermediaries or by proxy. During the present century this sort of approach has been attempted without any success in many political conflicts between nation-states. The long delay in the recognition of the Soviet Union between the two world wars, and the exclusion of

China from the United Nations for a quarter of a century after 1948, are perhaps the most conspicuous cases of a divorce between diplomacy and reality. If TNCs not only exist but are so powerful that, according to some, they are the tail that wags the dog, then TNCs must be recognized as important elements in international power relations and must be dealt with accordingly.

Perhaps, instead of undermining the concept of national sovereignty, the recognition of TNCs by the international community would not only help to solve some of the conflicts arising from their presence, but might also help to better define the extent and the limitations of the concept of sovereignty from the viewpoint of the interests of both the individual nation-states and the community of nations.(21) It is clearly up to the experts in international law to search for and, if necessary, invent legal formulas adequate for ensuring worldwide recognition of transnational corporations as international actors; the present muddle on the issue of TNC rights and obligations vis-a-vis nation-states is not particularly helpful for the NIEO.

Two major groups of nation-states continue to defend various myths with respect to TNCs. On the one hand, the developed countries in which transnationals originate and which provide the base for their activities claim that they do not have enough power to deal with these omnipresent entities. On the other hand, the developing countries, whose power is infinitely less than that of the developed countries and which are affected more than anyone else by TNC operations, adopt the position that TNC power can hopefully be curtailed by some sort of legally binding international covenant, which the TNCs would obey in spite of not being a party to it.

Both positions are difficult to defend. While the developed countries do have a lot of power over their TNCs, this power is limited by, among other things, the concept of national sovereignty so dear (for good reasons) to the weaker nation-states. At the same time, it seems highly unlikely that the power of the developing countries over TNC activities in their territories will increase merely through an international, legally binding agreement, unless provisions are made for its implementation. Legal measures without power of implementation are useless in the real world. Since the implementation of an agreement among nation-states on TNCs would, in many important instances, transcend national borders, no agreement on the future behavior of TNCs can be implemented without the participation of all parties concerned. The way in which TNCs will participate in the NIEO is a problem not yet satisfactorily explored. It is as crucial to the NIEO, however, as the participation of the socialist countries in the negotiations.

The Principle of Interdependence

The interdependence between the NIEO and the other global issues identified above has been recognized in some theoretical writings, but has not been reflected in the practice of national policy makers. Within the international public system this recognition has recently given rise to a stream of general declarations by consensus, solemn unilateral or group statements, and world "plans of action" whose practical value is extremely limited. In some circles, particularly in the North, such general declarations are often accompanied by a call to postpone any action with respect to the NIEO because other important things – such as big-power military and security problems – must be dealt with first. It has been repeated over and over again that once a major advance has been achieved between the West and the East on the issue of disarmament, then there will be time to take care of the NIEO, and only then will large resources be available for the solution of the global problem of underdevelopment.

The recognition of the interrelation between East-West armaments race and the failures of the NIEO may be of some assistance to the developing world. It helps to realize that while without progressive East-West detente there cannot be any major progress on the NIEO front, both roads should be followed simultaneously. Consequently, any developing country or group of countries which willingly plays upon or uses for its short-term benefits military and political tensions between the capitalist and socialist blocs damages the prospects for changes in economic relations between North and South. On the other hand, any developing country which diversifies its political and economic links, whether with the developed or with the developing countries, contributes in the long run to the NIEO by diffusing the bipolar power system and strengthening the trend toward a plurality of development models. In other words, an increased degree of rational dynamism in East-West relations, which depends not only on the superpowers and their respective allies but on the LDCs as well, might be of great use for NIEO purposes. It may be of assistance toward unfreezing the present apparently non-negotiable situation on specific NIEO issues.

Once it is recognized that the NIEO cannot progress in the climate of military tensions between East and West, it is not difficult to realize that any accommodation and conflict resolution, even partial, with respect to other global issues – nationalism, the distribution of profits of TNC activities, and sovereignty – would also represent a net gain for the NIEO.

Proponents of the NIEO raise with some frequency the question of whether the NIEO should be negotiated in a package or in parts. Some maintain that multilateral package negotiations are easier both for the developed countries and the developing countries because they offer tradeoffs between possible gains and losses involving specific issues and particular groups of nation-states. But the failure of the Paris CIEC undermines the validity of the "package deal" approach, not because the conference ended in failure but because the reasons for the failure cannot be ascribed exclusively to the developed countries.

A multilateral international negotiation of many issues can be successful only if a reasonable combination of tradeoffs is perceived and accepted, not only by the principal negotiating groups but by each major group of negotiating States. In Paris, while the industrial West demonstrated little if any interest in compromise solutions on individual items and on the package as a whole, the developing countries for their part showed little willingness to balance among themselves possible gains and losses accruing to their different subgroupings from different parts of the package.

All rhetoric notwithstanding, the degree of disagreement on the major NIEO issues among the developing countries (disguised by ingenious negotiating formulas), was no less than that which prevailed among the advanced countries. Internal disagreement has haunted the Group of 77 after the Paris Conference in its periodic negotiations on many specific issues, including the Integrated Programme for Commodities and the question of indebtedness. The persistence of these disagreements, which were relatively easy to sweep under the carpet of the "common front" in Paris in face of the rigid positions adopted by the leading developed countries, represents perhaps the biggest single threat to the future of the NIEO. The threat is compounded by the uncomfortable fact that the campaign of some industrialized Western countries to question the real existence of the Third World gains adherents in the newly industrialized developing countries.

Meaningful, multilateral "package" negotiations with the participation of over 100 nation-states are impossible not only politically but from the viewpoint of the logistics of the negotiating process. Moreover, if one considers the difficulty in defining and in agreeing upon the tradeoffs within the Group of 77, and the additional difficulty, faced by the theoretically equal sovereign co-actors, of delegating negotiating authority to others, one is left with the next best solution – the separate negotiation of the major NIEO issues in different fora.

There is no doubt that in such disjointed negotiations the developing countries are strongly handicapped by the limitations of their technical capacity at national levels. Therefore, the Group of 77 needs for its NIEO negotiations a secretariat similar to that of the OECD. Such a secretariat is useful, however, only if accompanied by an improved performance by the international public system, particularly the secretariats of the U.N.

An improvement of the U.N. performance should not be understood as an abandonment of its universality and impartiality but as the restoration of the system's only valid function: that of a competent intermediary in high conflict situations involving the majorities and minorities of the member-states. In the absence of innovative actions fostered by the U.N. and other international public agencies – actions that would strengthen the negotiating capacity of the developing countries and, at the same time, improve the role of the secretariat as an "honest middleman" – the U.N. system runs a double risk: first, of losing whatever international relevance it may still have, and, second, of transforming itself into an aimless conglomeration without any power to influence world development. The dangers of such a drift towards international irrelevance and oblivion should not be underestimated, particularly by those at the top of the international public system.

Any serious debate on the NIEO and its future must not limit itself to the repetition of earlier debates on the pros and cons of specific technical solutions for specific substantive issues arising from traditional economic relations between North and South. Such debate must occupy itself with the issues underlying the present deadlock and the progressive stagnation of the negotiations. It is not enough to agree that the issues are complicated and the negotiations difficult, and that it may take many decades to adjust the present economic order to the changing political order and to the rapidly increasing needs of the world's backward peripheries.

It is time to acknowledge that, while the NIEO is necessarily a complicated, difficult and drawn-out process, it will not be achieved – given the present pace of the negotiations – even by the end of the 21st century. This is not, however, to deny that some form of change is inevitable. Between 1875 and 1975 the world has changed most dramatically despite all sorts of obstacles arising from the teachings of conventional wisdom and from the short-term interests of the actors present on the international scene. Not only is there no doubt that the world will change again by the year 2075, but there are reasons to believe that the change will be even more profound than that which occurred in the past 100 years. While present attempts to promote the NIEO may make the process of change less unruly, less painful, and more rational, the obstruction of the NIEO will not stop change, as long as one does not equate change itself with the 19th century liberal idea of unending progress.

SUMMARY

The list of major issues underlying the present difficulties of the NIEO negotiations – issues to which more attention should be dedicated – includes the following:

a) the interdependence between the NIEO and other global issues;
b) the absence, for all intents and purposes, of the socialist countries from the NIEO negotiations;
c) the inclusion of TNCs as powerful international actors in the NIEO framework;
d) the relationship between East-West military and security conflicts and the NIEO;
e) the form of future negotiations, especially the package as opposed to the issue-by-issue approach; and
f) the declining efficiency and relevance of the international public system.

NOTES

(1) Among the relevant recent books one may mention Jagdish N. Bhagwati, ed., The New International Economic Order: The North-South Debate (Cambridge: The M.I.T. Press, 1977) and Karl P. Sauvant and Hajo Hasenpflug, eds., The New International Economic Order: Confrontation of Cooperation between North and South (Boulder, Colorado: Westview Press, 1978).

(2) One of the earliest but still one of the best contributions on the NIEO, a report of a group of experts appointed by Commonwealth Heads of Government at their meeting in Kingston, Jamaica in May 1975, identified major issues of the New International Economic Order: commodity arrangements; trade liberalization and access to markets; economic cooperation among developing countries; food production and rural development; industrial cooperation and transfer of technology; the transfer of resources; invisibles; and international institutions. For details, see Toward a New International Economic Order, Commonwealth Secretariat, (London: Malborough House, August 1975).

(3) Dragoslav Avramovic, The history of negotiations through UNCTAD IV can be found in "Commodities in Nairobi," Development and Change 8, no. 2: (April 1977): 231-248.

(4) An Associated Press cable from Geneva, published in International Herald Tribune (Paris) on Dec. 13, 1978 and quoted here in its entirety, describes well the situation prevailing in this field: "Nations that produce and consume natural rubber failed after four weeks of negotiations in Geneva to reach an international trade agreement. The United States was blamed for the impasse, and a U.S. official conceded "it is fair" to say Washington prevented an accord. Separately, in London, talks on a revised international pact for cocoa were also at an impasse with the United States apparently taking a hard line."

(5) For a quite realistic appraisal of the present trends in North-South trade see a speech of Olivier Long, Director General of GATT, before the European-Atlantic group (London), November 7, 1978, GATT Press Release 1223. According to Long, "four years of recession and stagnation were necessary to make people understand the degree to which the markets of the developing countries contribute to sustain the industrial activity in the developed countries. . . .There is the need now to translate this novel recognition into a more energetic change of the North-South relations."

(6) See, among others, Gerald K. Helleiner, "Manufactured Exports from Less Developed Countries and Multinational Firms," The Economic Journal (Oxford), no. 329, March 1973.

(7) Miguel S. Wionczek, ed., LDC External Indebtedness and the World Economy (Mexico: El Colegio de Mexico and CEESTEM, 1978).

(8) For details, see several contributions to World Development (Oxford), special issue dedicated to the LDC external indebtedness, January 1979.

(9) Dragoslav Avramovic, "Developing-Developed Country Negotiations: Recent Experience and Future Prospects," OPEC Review (Vienna), June 1978, p. 54.

(10) Miguel S. Wionczek, "Prospects for the UNCTAD Code of Conduct for the Transfer of Technology," Mazingira (Oxford), no. 8, 1979.

(11) Constantine V. Vaitsos, "Crisis in Regional Economic Cooperation Integration among Developing Countries: A Survey," World Development, (Oxford) 6, no. 6 (June 1978): 719-770.

(12) Karl P. Sauvant, "The Poor Countries and the Rich – a Few Steps Forward," Dissent (New York), Winter 1978, p. 54.

(13) A paper by I.H. Abdel-Rahman, "North Africa and Middle East: Economic and Political Issues," presented to this conference, notes that the general feeling one gets in that region is that the countries individually and collectively have many pressing problems of their own and would therefore spare little attention to the new international order as proposed globally. This observation is applicable to the rest of the underdeveloped world as well.

(14) Robert W. Gregg, Obstacles and Opportunities in the Establishment of the NIEO in the Field of Decision-Making Structure and Processes of the United Nations (Resume of a paper submitted to this conference), p. 4.

(15) W. Arthur Lewis, The Evolution of the International Economic Order, Research Program in Development Studies, Woodrow Wilson School, Discussion Paper, no. 74, Princeton University, Princeton, New Jersey, March 1977 (mimeo).

(16) On the immediate prospects of the world economy, see among others, UNCTAD, Interdependence of Problems of Trade, Development Finance and the International Monetary System – World Economic Outlook, 1978-1979, Geneva, TD/B/712, August 17, 1978. Moreover, not only are the developed countries' growth targets being revised downward continually, but the same is taking place in the socialist part of Europe. The growth rates for the USSR, Czechoslovakia, and Poland are expected to be, in 1979, 5.1 percent, 4.9 percent and 2.8 percent respectively, as against 10 percent or more a year in the previous quarter century.

(17) See, among others, United Nations, Updated Report of the Secretary-General, Economic and Social Consequences of the Arms Race and of Military Expenditure, 1978.

(18) See the Stockholm International Peace Research Institute (SIPRI) annual surveys on world armaments and arms trade. The interest in "national military independence" is not necessarily limited to rightist military governments. A recent report from Greece may be enlightening as it refers, among other things, to the political platform of the Panhellenic Socialist Party of Andreas Papandreou: "Greece already produces a great part of the ammunition it needs, and by the end of the year will be assemblying its own armoured personnel carriers. Missile-carrying motor-vessels are being built under license from the French. . . . If and when Mr. Papandreou comes to power, he promises that Greece will produce at least 80% of its armaments." "A survey of Greece," The Economist (London), December 16-22, 1978, p. 67.

(19) See "Comecon's Consuming Lust," The Economist (London), December 9, 1978, pp. 81-82.

(20) Miguel S. Wionczek, "Prospects for the UNCSTD – Three Underlying Issues," The Bulletin of the Atomic Scientist (Chicago), January 1979.

(21) See Raymond Vernon, "Multinationals: No strings Attached," Foreign Policy (Washington, D.C.), no. 33, Winter 1978-79 pp. 121-134.

4 Structural Obstacles to the NIEO from a Systems Analytic Viewpoint*

Vladislav B. Tikhomirov, Unitar

According to the special program adopted by the U.N. General Assembly, some difficulties related to the establishment of the New International Economic Order (NIEO) could be resolved through a fundamental restructuring of the world economic system. The structural obstacles to the NIEO, as well as the corresponding opportunities, must first be examined if we are to formulate a basis for radical decision making in this field.

Our analysis will be made in terms of the methodology of systems analysis. From this point of view there are different approaches to the structure of the system of the world economy and to the structure of other systems which are to be taken into account in considering structural obstacles to the NIEO. The examination of these different approaches is very important. But first it will be useful to say a few words about systems analysis itself.

A definition of systems analysis is difficult because it has several meanings which vary from one field of its application to another, from one author to another. For purposes of the present study, systems analysis may be viewed as a way of systematically examining complex problems under conditions of uncertainty, using a special method and procedure. The systems approach may be viewed as a set of methodological principles for the examination of complex and difficult problems. Our experience has shown that systems analysis could be very useful in assisting decision makers to define objectives and to formulate policies for achieving them.

From the viewpoint of systems analysis each research object has to be examined as a system. But specialists in this field usually hold that systems analysis itself begins only when the structure of the system is the object of consideration, taking into account the definition of structure as law of links and relations among elements of the system

---

*The opinions expressed here are those of the author and not necessarily those of UNITAR or any other organization with which he has been affiliated.

and among relationships of these elements. Many issues related to the establishment of the NIEO could be decided much more easily if specialists in this field would take into account this definition of structure.

From this point of view there are two different approaches to each structure. There is first the principle of <u>structural duality</u> of complex systems: in these systems two kinds of structures have to be taken into account – a structure of the system's elements, and a structure of <u>relationships</u> among the elements.

This approach can be useful in considering, for example, the structure of the world economic system or of national economic systems. The study of the structure of the economic system of a developing country is connected, for example, with the study of the structure of the system of elements of the economic system, and the structure of the system of relationships among these elements.

According to the Programme of Action on the Establishment of the NIEO, adopted by the General Assembly, the necessity of urgent and effective measures to assist the developing countries is connected in the first place with severe economic imbalances in the relations between developed and developing countries. From our point of view (see figure 4.1) one of the most important tasks of the NIEO is to improve the <u>structure of the system of relations</u> among the elements of the world economy, especially between the world capitalist economic system and the economic system of the Third World.

There is a contradiction between the structure of the system of elements of the world economic system (related to the new position of developing countries in the world system after their political de-colonization) and the structure of the system of relationships among elements of the world economic system (related to the archaic structure of the system of economic relationships among capitalist developed countries, and to the necessity of the social and economic decolonization of developing countries). Both of these structures are now inadequate. Thus, one of the most important obstacles to the establishment of the NIEO is connected with the present structure of the system of international economic relationships.

The capitalist developed countries are responsible for this situation because they took much from developing countries in previous years, and because they have been promoting the preservation of the structure of the system of capitalist relationships inside and outside the developing countries. There are now difficulties in the world capitalist economic system and in the economic system of the Third World, but the capitalist countries want, first of all, to pass their own difficulties on to the developing countries instead of offering better assistance to them.

With this in mind the difference between the measures of responsibility of capitalist and socialist countries for the present condition of the world economic system, and for the difficulties of developing countries, can be much more easily understood, For instance, the concept of interdependence must be examined without taking into

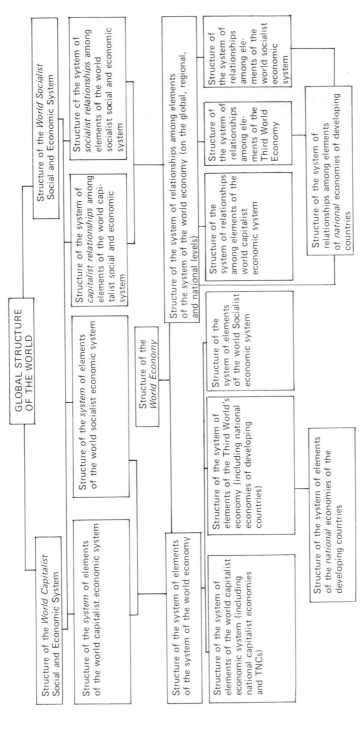

Fig. 4.1. Chart derived from internal UNITAR sources.

account the socialist developed countries' active attempts to amelio-
rate the basic difficulties of the present structure of the system of
international relations of developing countries, because these difficulties are not connected with the whole system of the world
economy. They are the result of the deep crisis of the world capitalist
social and economic system. They are in the field of economic
relationships between the world capitalist economic system and the
developing countries.

In considering the structure of the world economic system we do
have to take into account the role of the socialist countries, but only in
relation to one part of this structure: the structure of the system of
elements of the world economic system, since the socialist countries
are important elements in the world system. But the concept of
interdependence touches upon the second part of the structure of the
world economic system, which is connected with other laws of links and
relations in the system.

There is no interdependence between the system of relationships
with the participation of the socialist countries, and the system of
relationships among capitalist and developing countries because these
two systems require different approaches. Relationships between
socialist and developing countries are connected with the specific
structure of the system of these relationships, related to the specific
structure of the world socialist social and economic system.

One of the obstacles to the establishment of the NIEO arises from
attempts to examine the difficulties of developing countries without a
correct understanding of the differences between two basic approaches
to the structure of the system of relationships between developing and
developed countries; that is, without taking into account specific
features of the world socialist social and economic system on the one
hand, and the world capitalist social and economic system on the other,
which influence the international economic relations of developing
countries.

As elements of the world system, the socialist countries are
interested in a stable world economic system based on principles of
equality, justice, mutual benefit, and broad international relations. So
they support the ideas of the NIEO in principle and take part in United
Nations activities in this field. These countries are interested in the
development of their economic relations with other countries, but only
on a democratic and juridical basis, taking into account two different
approaches to these relations.

According to the program of action on the establishment of the
NIEO, the current difficulties of developing countries are connected not
only with the field of international economic relations. There is also the
constant and continuing aggravation of the imbalance of the economies
of the developing countries. There are some structural obstacles as
well, including the necessity to improve the structure of the system of
relationships among elements of national economic systems of the
developing countries, and sometimes the structure of the system of
elements of their economic systems. These obstacles are to be exam-

ined taking into account both economic and social issues, and the specific situation of each developing country.

It would be wrong to say that the principal obstacles in the developing countries lie only in the system of economic relationships among elements of the national economies of these countries. These obstacles are not connected with inequalities related only to the production sectors of developing economics. The distribution sectors are very important also, taking into account the structure of the social and economic systems of developing countries.

The structure of the system of elements of national social and economic systems can be improved for better distribution of power as well as for a corresponding reduction of inequalities. The best means to these ends are connected with progressive democratic transformations in the developing countries. The structure of the system of relationships among elements of national systems is to be taken into account for purposes of decision making related to issues of participation. The conditions of developing countries can be improved only on the basis of broad, structural reforms inside of the countries. An additional possible benefit would be the improvement of the structure of the system of relationships in the system of developing countries.

The development of international relations may be preferable for some developing countries to fundamental social and economic changes, because dominant groups in these countries influence decision making related to development. Sometimes these groups are not interested in changes of the structure of the system of elements, or in the new structure of the system of relationships inside these countries.

This obstacle is to be taken into account. The reasons for it may vary. Sometimes it arises from an incorrect understanding of the current situation in developing countries or from a poor perception of their needs related to development.

There is a very interesting feature of the term "new international economic order," related to the importance of structural changes related to two definitions which are often used — in this case "order" and "structure." They are closely interrelated because an "order" is a set of rules which affects links and relations in the system, and "structure" is viewed as a "law of links and relations" in the same field. Perhaps "order" touches only upon the system of relationships among elements of the basic system and "structure" is a broader definition related to the system of elements. Thus the NIEO could be considered a "new structure of the systems of economic relations," or a new set of rules related to the "new system of economic relations of developing countries."

This approach could help foster better understanding of the objectives of the NIEO as well as of the obstacles and opportunities related to its establishment, because from this point of view the most important obstacles are structural and are connected with improving the structure of the system of economic relations. The radical changes in this field (directed to the establishment of a new structure of the system of international economic relationships, one that is adequate as a modern structure of the system of elements of the world economic system) may be effective enough if they have a legal and institutional character rather than a commercial one. From this point of view one of the most important objectives of the NIEO consists in the necessity to improve the legal bases of international economic relations, especially international regulations of foreign trade with the participation of the developing countries, as well as the rules of their economic relations with capitalist developed countries and with TNCs.

Thus, for example, the most important issues of the world economy among the 25 areas enumerated by E. Laszlo and his collaborators in The Objectives of the NIEO are institutional and political:

a) assuring the economic sovereignty of states;
b) establishing a system of consultations at global, regional, and sectoral levels (not to be connected in all cases with the aim of promoting industrial development).

Among the other 22 issues of the world economy several are also connected with legal problems. They are to be taken into account earlier than others, particularly:

c) achieving a more equitable distribution of income;
d) regulating and supervising the activities of transnational enterprises;
e) establishing mechanisms for the transfer of technology to developing countries;
f) reforming the international monetary system (using special drawing rights);
g) assuring adequate participation by developing countries in decision making related to international financial issues;
h) improving the terms and conditions of trade of developing countries; and
i) improving and intensifying trade relations between countries having different social and economic systems.

The issue of undertaking "special measures to assist land-locked, least-developed and island-developing countries" is among the most important issues too, but there a difference in definition exists because this issue touches upon actors who take part in international relations, while all other issues are connected with a structural approach.

In conclusion, some words are needed in relation to the systems' behavior in terms of systems analysis. All systems which are to be considered in the establishment of the NIEO may be represented in dynamic terms; that is, in the process of their dialectical development. There are rules of behavior for these systems, including rules of stability or dynamic balance.

The structure of the system of elements of the social and economic systems may influence their stability, which is connected with the distribution of power among the elements. For an explanation of the existing conditions of the world economic system (as well as the corresponding obstacles) it would be important to take into account the rules of dynamic balance of this system, which are reflected in the structure. Contradictions related to the infringement of these rules are one of the important reasons for the current world economic situation. The behavior of the system can be limited by its structure. So, for example, the behavior of the world economic system is limited on certain frontiers by the existing character of the structure of the system of elements and the structure of the system of relationships among these elements. For a better understanding of this approach it is necessary to take into account two different kinds of structures (the second principle of structural duality): the invariant structure, and the state structure (this was discussed in our study related to the modeling of the world multi-system).(1) In the process of development the invariant structure should be represented by the invariant features of the behavior of the system in any period of time under consideration, but any new state of the system is connected with a new state structure (see figure 4.2). The state structure is a concretization of the general law reflected by the invariant structure.

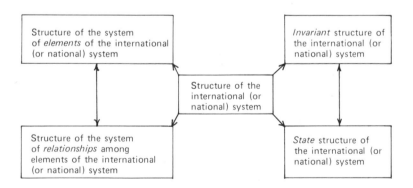

Fig. 4.2. Chart derived from internal UNITAR sources.

The necessity of the NIEO may be represented as a result of fundamental changes in the state structure of the world economic system. This is to be translated into qualitative conditions. The developing countries can aspire to change the state structure only by taking into account limitations related to the invariant structure and, of course, to the historic and social class approach to the study of social and economic systems.

NOTES

(1) V. Tikhomirov, Modeling of Multistate Dynamic Systems: New Approach and Application for Study of the World Structure, 6th Global Modeling Conference, IIASA, Vienna, October 1978.

5 The Function of International Law in the New International Economic Order

K. Venkata Raman,
Kingston, Ontario

The call for a new international order – an order that is more responsive to global needs and particularly to the needs of development – has in many ways begun to affect the foundations of international law on which the existing laissez-faire international economic system has traditionally based much of its authority. The demands for a new order represent but one facet of the larger global process of change, which has been proceeding especially vigorously since the signing of the Charter of the United Nations. The response at the international level of the NIEO claims cannot but have far-reaching implications for world public order.(1)

The concerted effort to achieve radical changes is not limited, however, to the management of the global wealth but extends to several other areas of vital human concern, such as the promotion of international peace and security, the protection of basic human rights, and the preservation of environmental quality. No perceptive observer of the contemporary international scene can fail to notice how, within the short period of three decades, perspectives of authority and control which shape and give effect to the policies of the world public order system have been dramatically altered in just about every field of international concern. Decolonization, detente, and development are no longer merely political slogans. They have become the staples of contemporary international practice and a major preoccupation of the United Nations. These developments have already begun to have their impact on the substantive content of international law.

Despite a growing awareness of the tremendous interdependencies conditioning the options of people everywhere, the global community, struggling to operate on the basis of the admittedly outmoded nation-state philosophy, is suddenly exposed to the task of managing problems which have defied effective solution on a formal basis. It is confronted with a challenge to devise new structures for collaboration which can appropriately accommodate all the diverse interests involved, and to create new policies for cooperation which are responsive to the differing needs and capabilities of the members.(2)

The adequacy of the present efforts to establish a new international economic order must be appraised in this global perspective. International lawyers accustomed to using conceptions of law as legitimizing factors appearing only after changes are well established, naturally find it difficult to rationalize and clarify either the purport of the new claims or the significance of the emerging identifications and expectations of the international community. Consequently it comes as no surprise that some of the most vocal, and admittedly weighty, objections to the formulated goals and aspirations of the NIEO are made in the name of international law. The purpose of this chapter is to briefly identify, first, the nature of the various types of claims surrounding the NIEO; second, obstacles to their implementation in the absence of clear agreement on the part of the developed countries; and third, the role law can play to promote both economic development objectives and economic security goals in a manner conducive to the common interests of all concerned.

Traditional considerations of reciprocity or mutuality of interest, which are believed to be the sustaining force behind all stable international economic transactions, have proven to be inadequate to equitably sustain economic relationships not marked by a reasonable degree of reciprocity. The function of legal principles in such situations is to provide a certain degree of regulatory authority to help promote such equity. Not all the NIEO claims, as is well known, present clear instances of reciprocal rights and obligations, in the sense in which international practice normally sustains a clear authority as to what is legally required or enforceable by the public authority of the international community. Foreign aid, technology transfer, avoidance of waste, and providing preferential terms of trade are some of the claims currently made at the international level for which the relevant policies are either unclear or not established as legally enforceable obligations. In those areas an effective NIEO must rest upon new prescriptions of international law. In yet other areas, especially those involving transnational corporations, the proper implementation of any agreed economic, political, and legal principles would also require new national legislation in order to be effective. Consequently, the attempt to create a new international economic order, to be effective, must also concern itself with procedures and mechanisms which are appropriate to the types of issue involved and the kinds of legal functions necessary for their management.

In addition, the task of a proper and effective management of even those NIEO issues on which there is clear consensus appears formidable because of the conflicting belief about which economic system is preferable, or should prevail, in order to carry out the agreements. The liberal market economies view the NIEO as a frontal attack upon the free market, nondiscriminatory laissez-faire system. On the other hand, the centrally planned economic systems perceive the unregulated market system as essentially favoring the western developed countries.

Some element of voluntary control and planning is essential, in their view, to correct the admittedly one-sided monetary system that has bred economic disequilibria and resulted in inequitable resource consumption.

The role of law in resolving these differences is sometimes perceived to be inadequate if not totally irrelevant. In a leading critique of the NIEO efforts, Ernst Petersmann echoed the concern of the developed industrialized states:

> As long as the OECD States consider the NIEO concept as an assault on fundamental principles of existing international economic law (nondiscrimination, reciprocity, market economy, freedom of property, and contract), the role of international law as a legal basis for international development aid will remain small (cf. the non-binding character of the UNCTAD system of preferences, and the lack of noncontractual legal obligations for development aid) and world economic reforms will continue to be tackled on a de facto basis. . . . Similarly the success of the . . . Charter. . .will depend on a diminution of the legal and economic divergences between industrial nations and developing countries.(3)

What are those "fundamental principles of international economic law" which stand in the way of a NIEO? Which of the stated NIEO objectives constitutes a serious threat to the common interest conveyed by those principles? Assuming that some do, is it not possible to clarify where precisely lies the common interest, given a genuinely shared perception of the increasingly obvious interdependence among developed and developing states?

Such a policy clarification, it has been asserted, is not possible as long as international legal principles governing global economic transactions continue to operate in the manner in which they have during a period of overseas economic exploitation of the resources and services of colonies. Indeed, legal scholars from the developing countries question even the juridical premises upon which the system of international economic law has been built, and advocate a radical reformation of these legal concepts.(4) Concepts of private ownership were applied to the property controlled by transnational corporations in the extractive industries. Not only the fixed assets and mining structures in which they made financial investments, but the natural resources of the host countries became, until the expiration of the period stipulated in the concessions (often extending over several generations!), property owned by the foreign investor. Such ownership included exclusive control over the production, processing, and marketing of the particular resource. Even after their political independence, the developing countries, because of the nature and scope of the investor ownership (tied to control over markets and the supply of technology), remained, for all practical purposes, only the nominal possessors of their property. Indeed, after their nationalization, developing countries often had to continue to rely upon and consult the same foreign corporations, forsaking effective control in order to extract the full value of their resources and implement long-term economic development programs.

Because natural resources acquire economic value only when brought into the marketplace, the institution of contract remains the major tool governing relations between the foreign investor and the host state. The sanctity of contract is derived from the basic postulate pacta sunt servanda — that agreements should be observed in good faith. The notion that long-term developmental arrangements concerning a basic natural resource of a state (perhaps its only major resource) is a species of private law of contract, has defied, it is said, rational accommodation of the competing objectives of the two sides to the agreement. While the options open to the territorial sovereign appear to be focused on a seemingly beneficial joint venture or outright nationalization, the corresponding options to achieve their objectives open to the TNCs have been in fact quite varied and extensive. Intracorporate pricing practices, restrictions on the availability of technology and its exorbitant costs, manipulations of the international markets, and fixing of the prices of commodities are some of the well-known devices employed.

So fundamental and deeply entrenched are the differing perspectives among the few developed and the many underdeveloped member states of the United Nations that the task ahead is appropriately perceived by those responsible for steering fruitful negotiations as requiring "the building of a new and better world. . .somewhat different from the one that history bequeathed us, in which a few countries dominate the rest of the world."(5)

The suggestion has been made that if most of the NIEO claims involve zero-sum demands (i.e., if A's benefit entails B's loss), efforts should be directed to transforming the underlying demands into non-zero-sum situations so that rational agreement in the near future would become possible.(6) Obviously where there is room for tradeoffs, bargaining, or bartering, trade practices can quickly pick up momentum. Once established, the practices of international trade naturally entrench themselves as authoritative, and are recognized as such by international legal tribunals.(7) But, as mentioned above, the great number of issues involved in the claim to establish a NIEO cannot be left simply to "private settlements."

Unfortunately, in management of the global wealth process public decision makers have hitherto been generally content with nominal, supervisory functions. International jurisprudence remained bereft of any "global welfare" prescriptions.(8) International law can perform a useful regulative as well as corrective function in the economic process without jeopardizing the basic preferences or individual initiatives of the main actors. The argument often advanced by the industrialized market economies to the effect that they cannot regulate the activities of transnational corporations even when certain activities in which they are engaged are patently deprivational in effect, betrays the persistence of the dominant ethic in global relationships.

Nor is the NIEO package in any sense limited in its scope to merely regulating the prerogatives of foreign investors. The traditional legal premises for granting protection to the proprietary interests of aliens against discrimination or unjust deprivation are not any less important or relevant to the developing countries today. For the great majority of the newly independent developing countries, who are genuinely interested in maintaining an equitable and just international economic order and increasingly conscious of the fact that soon some of them will be exporters of technology and suppliers of foreign investment capital, it is not the fundamental juridical concepts of good faith, inviolability of private property, and protection of the corporate personality that are at issue. What is at issue is the blind determination with which policies inherited from a colonial economic context, and perpetuating unjust and untenable inequities, are affirmed as immutable principles of law. These are the laws that they challenge and desire to change, in the larger interests of achieving an inclusive and integrated global economic system.

Although the Programme of Action of the NIEO and related formulations emerging from the Sixth and Seventh Special Sessions of the General Assembly, together with the Charter of Economic Rights and Duties of States are the ones frequently cited as NIEO claims, in fact such claims extend over a wide range of issues, several of them the subjects of a number of communications which have emerged from the conferences held both within and outside the United Nations and affiliated international organizations over a period of two decades. In attempting to outline how international law is crucially important to the NIEO debates, this chapter will focus on five or six broad areas currently under discussion in various global economic conferences.

In the investigation of the key NIEO issues outlined below, the relevant question to be asked is not whether, or to what extent, international law is relevant for achieving the goals thus identified; obviously, the legal technique is an indispensible component of any international effort for achieving agreement, no matter in what particular form or modality it is applied. Rather, our concern is with the question of what facilitative opportunities, of an international law character, can be identified as goals to be achieved which could possibly assist in clarifying the common interests of both developing and developed states. In its most general sense the NIEO efforts have met with some fundamental objections of a conceptual character. Although they are philosophic in nature, they seem to influence the responses forthcoming on specific NIEO issues; therefore it is pertinent to deal briefly with them here.

PERCEPTIONS OF THE NIEO

Conflicting perceptions about the nature and purpose of NIEO demands have clearly polarized the contending groups, and it is widely felt that the negotiating framework, both within and outside the United Nations, has not been successful in promoting even mutual perceptions of common interests. For instance, it can be postulated that international trade and economic growth are possible only under conditions of sufficient legal security and free, nondiscriminatory access to resources. However, the majority of developing states, who are in need of appropriate modern technology and foreign capital, view the unstructured market system as placing them in a noncompetitive position, with all the attendant disadvantages. Their demands are not limited to making a few adjustments to the prevailing market mechanisms. They wish to raise such policy issues as: the imperatives of foreign aid and economic assistance, including direct foreign investment policies; the framework of international trade, including equitable and preferential trade mechanisms which balance favorably the costs and values of their natural resources vis-a-vis imported manufactures; the availability of appropriate technology; and their own ability to pursue economic developmental policies without adverse outside intervention. The call for a NIEO is identified with the needs of the developing countries to regain their right to exercise permanent sovereignty over their natural resources (that is, to exercise national control over private foreign investment in a manner conducive to the promotion of their economic development), and to enhance the flow of foreign capital through trade and aid. In other words, while one side is emphasizing free (nondiscriminatory) competition, protection of the market system based on such competition, and free access to the natural resources of the developing countries ("economic security," as it has been called), the other side advocates development going beyond the free market ethic, demanding an equitable share in the international division of labor.

Another element, and by far the most important dimension of the NIEO debate insofar as international law is concerned, is the role played by transnational corporations and the related question of rectifying the adverse effects of existing legal concepts and institutions on North-South relationships. In part because the "market forces" are largely, if not exclusively, controlled by giant transnational corporations based in a few industrialized nations, policies governing international trade and commerce have remained in the elusive domain of the invisible private corporate structure. Since these enterprises have been reluctant to transfer technology or institute processing industries in a manner beneficial to a balanced growth of the economies of the developing countries (because they may not yield maximum profits), policies concerning "sovereignty" over resources and other related issues have become a matter of bitter contention. The issues in conflict are not whether the transnationals play a critical role in the economic development of the developing countries. They do. But as participants in the global economic process, with the market as their arena and the maximization of private profit as their main objective, they have an important new role to play as agents in achieving NIEO goals. The Action Programme on the NIEO has focused attention on the need to "formulate, adopt and implement an international code of conduct for TNCs..." and "to eliminate restrictive business practices in whatever form present, adversely affecting international trade, especially that of the developing countries." There is general agreement on the overall objective of negotiating a set of equitable principles in these areas. Both the UNCTAD proposals and the OECD guidelines emphasize that certain TNC practices in restraint of trade should be eliminated, although the respective reasons why do not always appear identical.(9) The practices the OECD countries are interested in controlling are all related to maintaining a free and competitive market system. The type of activities the developing countries are interested in regulating also extend to intracorporate transactions, transfer pricing arrangements, technology transfer restrictions, market monopolies, and price-fixing practices. While the OECD countries prefer a voluntary code, the Group of 77 is seeking a set of legally binding principles. The overall framework for negotiation on these and other related issues, both within UNCTAD and in the U.N. Commission on Transnational Corporations, has been somewhat too formal and narrow. Despite the fact that a substantial part of the foreign investment capital, technology, and patents are neither the prerogative, nor within the control, of governments, but instead consist exclusively of property within the private sector monopolized by transnational enterprises, the latter do not yet have a direct participatory role in the formulation and development of NIEO policies and the procedures for their implementation.(10)

As the agenda of the "basic issues" (identified by the intergovernmental working group of the U.N. Commission on Transnational Corporations) amply demonstrates, there are a number of formidable problems whose resolution is dependent upon active cooperation between the industrialized and the developing countries. Such cooperation may take the form of either specific multilateral conventions or general principles recommended to states for inclusion in their bilateral agreements or contracts. But the most formidable, and by far the most controversial among the declared NIEO principles directly bearing on the role of private transnational enterprises, has been the concept of Permanent Sovereignty as articulated in Article 2 of the Charter of Economic Rights and Duties of States. There are three important issues involved in this concept which remain a major bone of contention between the two sides. These refer, in their broadest sense, to:

a) the nature and scope of the contractual undertakings affecting foreign investments and the legal principles governing their interpretation and application;
b) the treatment of property rights, including industrial property arrangements and the property value of the natural resources to which they are applied;
c) the openness and integrity of trading methods and practices, and the degree to which they may be subjected to a system of international law, irrespective of whether the trading units are private transnational corporations or state trading agencies.

These issues have historically been the subject of considerable international legal regulation. There is extensive jurisprudence and "state practice" behind many of the doctrines of <u>pacta sunt servanda</u> as applied to international trade and concession agreements. Many of the notions of "private property" have been applied to the protection of the foreign investor's property rights in natural resources subjected to concessionary regimes. The business practices of transnational enterprises are often shielded under the fiction that since a corporation has a "personality" of its own, no state can exercise its extraterritorial jurisdiction to its activities when these take place outside its territorial jurisdiction. The NIEO claims challenge some of these fundamental juridical assumptions.

LEGAL DIFFICULTIES OF THE NIEO PRINCIPLES

Critics of the NIEO also point out that, for the most part, formal principles emanating from the many conferences addressed to the issues of economic development of the developing countries lack balance and are one-sided: the NIEO speaks about the obligations of and concessions to be made by developed countries, and about the rights of developing countries, but not about their own corresponding duties and obligations.(11) According to this view, many of the formally declared principles are couched in terms of demands for imperative action without a systematic balancing of the wide range of rights and duties which such action might entail. It has been pointed out that this deficiency persisted even when the formulating sessions had the benefit of legal expertise, as was the case with the drafting of the Charter of Economic Rights and Duties of States. The criticism is not so much about infelicities in the drafting of the formal legal principles as about the adequacy of the substantive principles identified for the management of the process of global economic development.

All the relevant policies pertaining to a transaction, or relevant in a situation, merit equal treatment. Thus, for example, the critics are right when they point out that Article 2 of the Charter of Economic Rights and Duties of States (which defines the scope of the host state's competence to nationalize foreign investment and then describes the rights and obligations of the parties directly affected by such actions, but remains silent on the obligation of the parties to observe all provisions of a foreign investment agreement in good faith) is one-sided. The claim that the principle of good faith has already found expression in the cryptic itemization of Article 1 of the same Charter is not quite convincing or even helpful for resolving particular disputes between the two sides.(12)

The criticism that many of the claims advanced in the name of the NIEO suffer from lack of comprehensiveness, balance, and specificity, cannot be extended too far. The role of law in the management of transnational relations – more than in the management of domestic relations – is influenced largely by customary practices. Custom is not only the most democratic of the methods by which law is created, but it permits considerable flexibility in making changes in the main body of that law in order to take into account changes present in the social context to which it must respond if it is to be effective. It is thus understandable why developing countries were reluctant to use expressions such as "international law" or "international minimum standard" in the crucial provisions of Article 2 of the Economic Charter. The vast majority of the developing states project the NIEO as a demand for change of the existing international law. They view the law of international trade as a whole, and the doctrine of "state responsibility" insofar as it relates to international trade, as a law of laissez-faire favoring the industrialized states. Within the existing decentralized system of public order, changes in law can be achieved only by a radical departure from existing norms initiated by interested states. Any state that seeks to make new law cannot be expected to agree to litigate under the old law, for what it proclaims as new law will have to be received as violation of the old, unless a comprehensive treaty or convention, fully ratified and in force, is available to rebut the presumptions under which third-party decision makers often decide such disputes.(13) This is not to suggest that international law in general, and new perceptions of basic minimum international standards for the treatment of foreign property interests, are not relevant. Indeed, much of the debate during the UNCTAD preparatory meetings, in the working group entrusted with the drafting of the charter, was focused on the issue of whether the latter should take the form of a multilateral treaty or convention open to formal ratification, or remain a promotional exercise designed to influence future developments. The need to introduce specific changes in the content of minimum international standards for the treatment of foreign economic interests can be most clearly seen as a set of additional policy guidelines constituting a part of the minimum standard doctrine — which is in fact what appears to be the purpose of the charter itself.

Admittedly, this is a politically difficult task to achieve within the span of a few years. The tasks of policy enunciation in the requisite detail, and specification of the contingent fact situations affected by them, traditionally called codification and progressive development of law, cannot be achieved in full measure through such hastily organized conferences. As Richard Falk pointed out, "to make policy explicit in periods of change and confrontation is to rob law of its mystifying potency. Such an exposure generates subversive tendencies, however unintentionally, that undermine fixed patterns of respect, thinking, feeling and acting."(14) The reluctance of developing countries to invoke the protection of the principles of international law applicable to the changing circumstances of international economic relationships appears unfortunate. In consequence, a recent international arbitral decision concerned with interpreting and applying Article 2 of the charter came to the conclusion that "several factors contribute to denying legal value to those provisions of the document" and that "it must be analyzed as a political rather than as a legal declaration concerned with the ideological strategy of development and, as such supported only by non-industrialized States."(15)

Finally, the principal criticism that the NIEO process is not pegged to a mutually dependable third-party procedure for settlement of international economic disputes refers to the institutional basis of the projected new economic order. The reference to third-party settlement in the charter is dependent upon the consent of the parties involved in dispute. The ambivalence in the specification of the precise content of the international standard applicable under such procedures appears responsible, to some extent, for the omission of advance commitments to submit such disputes to third-party settlement. But this is not really germane; to a large extent the reciprocal interests of the parties involved appear to influence the options open to them to deviate radically from the economic regime initially envisaged, or to alter their agreed contractual relationship beyond bringing it into conformity with the new developments. Notwithstanding this, it appears to have been a tactical mistake on the part of the drafters of the charter not to have provided for a set of generally defined principles to govern the renegotiation of long-term investment agreements.

From a substantive point of view this deliberate omission of any reference to international standards must be seen as the result of two kinds of failure on the part of the international community. There is, first, the failure of international law to develop first-order principles for allocating an equitable share in global economic growth for raw material exporting developing countries; and, second, the failure of the industrialized, raw material importing developed countries and their TNCs to negotiate agreements for the establishment of institutions and procedures to deal on a regular and continuing basis with the problems of underdevelopment and inequitable distribution of the benefits in the international distribution of labor. The failure of international law to develop comprehensive, inclusive policies for the global economic process on the one hand, and the insistence with which it applies procedures and concepts borrowed from private national law to explain international trade relationships on the other, appears to be the reason why the charter is couched only in terms of the demands and expectations of developing states.

The foregoing survey of general objections of a conceptual character, which directly or indirectly influence the specific outcomes of particular NIEO issues, is by no means complete. It nevertheless underscores the nature and scope of the difficulties in achieving successful negotiations on many important issues where a measure of consensus may be possible. The North-South dialogue has moved from the era of declaration of goals to the era of negotiation of specific outcomes. Since the phase of petition is over, organized effort must be made for practical action which can transform the present relations of dependence into those of genuine partnership for the achievement of the common interests of both developing and developed countries.

THE GLOBAL WEALTH PROCESS: POLICIES IN
THE COMMON INTEREST

The conception of the international legal process most appropriate for the management of the international economic order may be described, in broadest terms, as one in which stability of authority and control characterizes economic relationships in which values (not limited to wealth alone) are shaped and shared more by persuasion than by coercion, to promote — as equitably as circumstances permit — the greatest production and the widest possible sharing of all values, among all human beings.(16) Obviously no public order system, whether at the local, regional, national, or global level, is ever able to achieve value shaping and sharing without imposing some measure of policing and regulatory control. Indeed, the functions of modern government in the most enduring democracies are largely devoted to devising and implementing social welfare policies which accord opportunities for value maximization to the segments of the population most in need of such support. Comparable welfare measures at the transnational level have been slow to emerge, despite many fervent calls by international organizations to establish mechanisms for promoting global equity and welfare. Inflated notions of national sovereignty have prevented the emergence of a comprehensive set of inclusive, international policies commanding the respect of both the developing and the developed segments of the global economic community.

In point of fact, the concept of "development," in its legal connotation as a tool for obligatory participation, is now in need of further clarification. The notions of contract fidelity and inviolability of foreign property rights are intimately related to the policy content of the legal obligations embraced by the notion of "development." Since the purpose of the NIEO is to rectify the historic "distributive injustices" which have characterized several centuries of economic "exploitation," the legal obligations governing the implementation of the NIEO objectives, and the legal basis of the developmental goals in general, must be made explicit. It is simply not enough to assert that the NIEO charters and resolutions are (or are not) legally binding instruments. The legal authority and significance of the NIEO principles have their juridical basis in the Charter of the United Nations, a document that is "legally binding" on every member state. Our concern should therefore be addressed to the particular aspects of the NIEO issues, and to the role international law can play in their realization. Even a brief shopping list of the critical issues involved in the claims to establish the NIEO reveals the magnitude and complexity of the problems, and the variety of legal techniques called for in their treatment.

1. Third world debts. Is it possible to generalize from current international practice a normative basis calling for an obligation to renegotiate third world debts? If general legal criteria can be based upon genuinely shared expectations created by the tendencies of governmental behavior since the adoption of the NIEO documents, would that not serve as an additional source of authority for the

propositions contained in the NIEO documents? What are the implications of such a definite, formal source of legal obligation for the future of the NIEO in contrast to the present ad hoc treatment method, advocated by the principal aid-donating countries? What is the overall approach of international institutions such as the IMF, IBRD, and IFC? The criteria of solvency applied by the international monetary institutions for determining the creditworthiness of developing countries, if determined solely on the basis of their balance-of-payments position, may result in onerous burdens with devastating social and political consequences.   Therefore, the policies of such institutions must be subject to inclusive, economic development oriented principles. In what form and strategy should such principles be set and declared?

2. The paucity of international law governing technical and financial aid. Both direct foreign investment arrangements and financial aid operations are usually affected by shifting governmental policies. On occasion, the shift may be the direct result of adverse political developments between the aid-giving and aid-receiving countries. Changes in economic and trade factors caused by policies of a third-party are also known to have adverse effects on the developmental programs of aid recipients. Often, domestic legislative practices and specific national legislations, not intended to affect a developing country, nevertheless jeopardize its economic development plans. Legislative measures undoubtedly within the exclusive domain of the aid-giving nations vary considerably. The international law of "state responsibility," a subject under extensive consideration of the International Law Commission, may be relevant here. (As a practical measure, a set of general principles addressed to this problem should perhaps be included for consideration by the International Law Commission.)

3. Legal rights and obligations governing transfer of technology. Technology transfer has both economic and social implications. The needs for appropriate technology and the obligation to provide it can be brought into balance with the proprietary interests of technology holders if the transactions are properly subjected to the shared perceptions of the two sides involved. Shelved technology has no real economic value, but taken off the shelf it could help in meeting the developmental needs of the technologically poor segments of the global economy. Its profitability can be a function of the larger prospects for collaboration its use can produce.

4. Legal issues related to international trade of Third World countries. This focuses on the present legal status of Most Favored Nation (MFN) treatment clauses in economic treaties and trade agreements. (More will be said below on the need to develop the notion of a "most favored developing nations treatment" concept.)

5. International law relating to tariff and non-tariff barriers on the exports of manufactures from the Third World. The interrelationship between this issue and those of redeployment, international labor, taxation, and domestic employment must be explored.

6. International legal regulation of shipping, transportation, insurance, and other elements in so-called invisible trade.

7. To what extent international law facilitates the exercise of the right of states to form "producers' associations," for achieving "just prices" and for the formation and management of "buffer stocks."

8. The role of international law in ensuring free access to world markets of products manufactured in the developing countries. This would be achieved by regulating the monopoly practices of transnational corporations.

9. Methods for establishing truly multinational corporations among the developing and raw material exporting countries, or for specific commodity-oriented areas that can promote global welfare objectives. Can such corporations achieve sufficient authority to make it profitable for them to stay in business?

10. The development of legal techniques for the regulation of restrictive business practices. Such practices include transfer pricing arrangements, consultancy contract, intracorporate tax distribution methods, and other, similar practices that have adverse effects on the resource value yielded to developing countries.

11. The right to permanent sovereignty over natural resources. Does the exercise of this right in accordance with the national policies, legislation, and procedures of the host country constitute invariably an "arbitrary discrimination" antithetical to the goal of promoting international cooperation? What are the legal impediments for the full exercise of "permanent sovereignty" by states not only over resources in situ but over all economic activities generated by such resources? Unlike the doctrine of "diplomatic protection" accorded to the foreign proprietary interests of transnational corporations, to exercise control over the transfer pricing policies of such corporations (especially when they affect the resource value accruing to the host state) are not proscribed by international law. The latter simply has not developed appropriate policies for treating such disputes.

12. Ocean and seabed resources. The impact of the NIEO on emerging policies for ocean mineral management is evident in the negotiations of the United Nations Conference on the Law of the Sea. Policies governing the unrestrained production of resources for common enjoyment, unimpeded access to technology, equitable distribution of the exploited resources, and price controls to protect land-based economies may offer a useful model for application to other areas, as well as provide sufficient impetus to bring about changes in customary international law.

13. The free choice by states of their domestic political and economic systems. The legal implications of this claim for seeking revision of the contractual and concessional obligations earlier entered into cannot be understood without looking into the political and social context of "change" in the relationships of states. Many of the "trading with the enemy acts" of the industrialized countries apply to their TNCs doing business with developing countries where the enemy may or may not be a common one. Less explicit restraints on TNCs by home

states may place unnecessary constraints on the economic development of the developing countries. Another pertinent dimension of this claim refers to the role of TNCs in the host countries' domestic affairs. Recent revelations of TNC involvement in internal political and social developments have underscored the magnitude of this problem.

14. Special measures to strengthen the developmental needs of landlocked, least developed, and island countries. How far are the rights of these countries protected by international law? If their rights are recognized internationally but the implementation of the rights is subject to individual agreement, how are they to be realized in practice? This is not merely a North-South but a South-South issue, since many of the land-locked developing countries (LLDCs) depend for their transit rights on their neighboring developing countries.

It is apparent that this list can be expanded to include claims from both sides, as well as other problem areas not perceived in the NIEO context but relevant to it. The list does not pretend to be a homogenous itemization of all issues involved in the current debates.(17) While the legal perspective is relevant to all of these issues, the most promising (and controversial) among them may be given special mention here.

Economic Aid, Outright Grants and Soft Loans, and the Servicing of Public and Private Debts

The Declaration and Programme of Action on the Establishment of a New International Order have identified a number of specific measures for facilitating the transfer of resources, and for maintaining stability in the value of currencies and exchange rates of major trading nations, to achieve balanced growth and economic development. A most conspicuous feature of postwar economic relationships is the important regulatory role played by international monetary institutions such as the IMF in the maintenance of stable exchange rates. National sovereignty and economic independence are thus voluntarily subjected to international agreements. The mechanisms of prior notice and consultation are designed to prevent excessive fluctuations and promote free transfer of resources to facilitate international trade and commerce in goods and services.(18)

The Programme of Action also refers to measures for preventing the adverse effects of inflation in developed countries from being transferred to developing countries, and for ensuring a greater role for the latter in decision making procedures of international financial institutions. Financial flows in real terms are no doubt a function of export capabilities as well as of sound national policies. Apart from specific policies underlying Official Development Aid (the target of 0.7 percent of GNP, set for the second development decade, having remained largely unattained), the need for borrowing stable foreign currencies to maintain the value of domestic currencies is hardly limited to developing countries alone. For example, during 1978-79, among the three largest borrowers in the Euro-dollar Market were Brazil, a rapidly industrializing developing country, and Canada, an industrialized developed one. Often lacking the ability to borrow in the open market, the developing countries are dependent upon "foreign aid" to augment their domestic resources, sometimes borrowing merely to service outstanding debts. Countries giving foreign aid are naturally sensitive to possible risks and tend to limit assistance to programs likely to strengthen the balance-of-payments position of the borrower. It is often emphasized that foreign investment should be so directed as to increase a country's exports or to decrease its imports. It is assumed that the investment will then act directly to strengthen the payments position as much as meet the additional exchange requirement to service the investment. Even if from a purely economic point of view the logic of the underlying assumptions was unassailable, from a social and political point of view such ramified foreign arrangements can have a negative impact. In a report prepared by the Center for International Policy of Funds for Peace, in Washington, the effect on human rights of the financial policies of the IMF have been noted.

> It is inconceivable that a government would be cut off from foreign capital because the poverty rate increased though a government is very much in danger of being cut off if its current accounts deficit has increased. Governments are 'judged' on the basis of their economic and financial transactions as related to foreign exchange and trade balances with the IMF acting as the major disciplinary agency. . . .(19)

After noting the close connections among poor working conditions, unrelieved labor grievances, and high unemployment, and specific responses of rank and file trade unionists that led to massive arrests and the breakdown of civic order in many developing countries, the report continues:

> Judging from the many military dictators seizing power and imposing harsh economic stabilization programmes in the highly indebted non-oil producing countries, it would seem that the only cure for debt, and certainly the one advocated by the banks, is to sacrifice internal well-being for external growth. It is more than ironic that international financial institutions should now be urging more effective policies to alleviate poverty when it has been their insistence on orthodox economic practices that has made alleviating poverty all but impossible.(20)

The supervisory functions of international monetary and financial agencies can be effective in policing extravagant state investment policies if the most fundamental aspects of global economic development policies are sufficiently clarified. Such an effort would, however, entail intruding into the jealously guarded domestic jurisdiction of all governments. Yet an international economic order concerned with human welfare cannot for long be oblivious to these problems.

Underlying many of the specific demands of the developing countries in the financial area is the emerging conception of foreign aid and aid preferences based on need. Such entitlement to aid is beginning to be recognized as an aspect of international responsibility on the part of the affluent members of international society. Such a notion influences the entire range of international decisions pertaining to economic development. Referring to the policies followed by OPEC countries in the matter of financial assistance to the developing countries adversely affected by the increase in oil prices, Dr. Shihata of Kuwait went on record to acknowledge a legal obligation to grant aid as an evolving principle of customary international law.(21)

As a broad consideration of development policy, the slow recognition of a concept of international entitlement to aid on the part of the capital-exporting states is bound to be an important factor in the evolution of the international law of development. The evidence for this comes not only from the recommendations of the U.N. Second Development Decade, but also from the recent actions of some of the rich countries in granting assistance and preferences to severely affected developing countries.(22) Indeed, policies underlying recent decisions to write off large amounts of the public debt of some developing countries apply with equal cogency to the arguments of the developing countries that calculations of "appropriate compensation," in the event of nationalization, must rest on the needs and the abilities of the host state to pay the full market value demanded by the foreign corporation or its protectors.(23)

Although the present rationale for extending international economic assistance is somewhat similar to the notions of the modern welfare state (the implications for international peace and security are obviously uppermost in such calculations), the entitlement of the developing countries to foreign aid does not appear to be affected by the fact that the recipients' needs arose in part because the donor countries vigorously objected to the specific economic policies which the recipients opted to pursue. Already by the time of the NIEO declaration, countries such as Ghana have invoked debt moratorium as an option in respect of their contractual obligations. (The scope of this emerging norm of international law is also examined by the International Law Commission in its draft report on "State Responsibility.")

In addition to the role of public international organizations, the servicing of the financial obligations incurred by developing countries raises important legal and policy questions involving both individual governments and private commercial banking institutions. The public and publicly guaranteed debt owed by developing countries at the end of 1977 reached a staggering $220-25 billion. The debt servicing position of the Group of 77 is certainly not uniform, and many important distinctions may have to be made even among the relatively poor countries. Among rapidly developing countries such as Brazil, Mexico, Korea, and India, debt servicing capabilities are intimately related to the ability to capture markets for manufactured goods.

The international trading regime offers, to some extent, a way out. But for the rest, debt servicing calls for more drastic reintegrating approaches. The recommendations of the 1979 UNCTAD Trade and Development Board may, where appropriate, also be made applicable to servicing the claims of private banking institutions. The major function of international law in this matter is to create stability in expectations about the availability as well as the accountability of capital flows.(24) A secondary function is to offer policy clarification for achieving tolerable adjustments in the areas of financial obligation and state responsibility arising out of contractual debts incurred from public as well as private sources.

International Trade, Access to Markets, Tariff Preferences, and Economic Development

A secure and mutually dependable framework for promoting inter-national trade must necessarily address itself to such institutionalized practices as the most-favored nation treatment (and if the nation that must be favored is the one most in need, a most favored developing nation treatment); preferential trade opportunities (the Generalized System of Preferences negotiated in 1979 favors OECD interests over those of the weaker trade partners); the removal of onerous tariff and non-tariff barriers (the much advertised showpiece, namely the EEC-ACP Lome Convention, is up for renewal when it expires in 1980); and the setting up of stable but equitable pricing policies for exports, especially of developing countries. Traditionally, international law has played an important regulatory role in many of these areas. But its application has been highly erratic and often discriminatory.

The postwar Bretton Woods arrangement, popularly known as the GATT system, has proved to be inadequate to meet many of the pressing demands of the developing countries. For one thing, the GATT system was envisaged to regulate international trade, which at that time was carried out largely by private corporate enterprises. With the advent of state trading, the practices of TNCs came into sharp conflict with the aspirations of the developing countries. The 1971 decision to let the major currencies float, followed by the OPEC pricing changes, led to the issue of indexation. The concept of "just price" for raw materials exported by developing countries is perceived to fall within the concerns of international law.(25)

A second major category of issues raised by the NIEO, which may also be broadly categorized as international trade questions, calls for making appropriate adjustments to facilitate the expansion and diversi-fication of Third World exports. Although the realization of this goal is seen as requiring cooperation at the intergovernmental level (for lower tariffs and for the removal of non-tariff barriers on the exports of manufactured goods originating from the Third World), major impedi-ments can be found in the restrictive business practices of TNCs, including their manipulation of the market structure and their influence upon labor and trade unions in industrialized countries. The whole area of transportation, insurance, and banking arrangements, referred to as "invisible trade," is very much controlled by the TNCs, and the Third World demands a role in these sectors as well.

Fundamental to the NIEO is a broadly agreed scheme of indexation of Third World export prices in a manner that would tie them to the rising prices of the manufactured goods and capital exported by the developed countries. Indexation in the international context has been shunned and criticized although the concept, or its functional equivalent, has been accepted in certain areas by developed countries. Closely related to indexation is the idea of adopting an integrated approach to price supports for an entire group of Third World commodity exports. It is argued that international trade under such a scheme would benefit from the creation of buffer stocks for which "producers' associations" are seen as a practical vehicle. Consequently a right of association for primary producers is demanded, and the developed countries are required not to prevent, in policy or practice, the organization of such trading centers. They are also called upon to finance, through a "common fund," the creation of buffer stocks for achieving stability in prices. We need only recall here that the attempts under the Havana Charter (1948) to establish an International Trade Organization have failed on the same issue of primary commodity policies and the role of cartels. Instead, the regulation of commodity prices is now attempted through international commodity agreements between producer and consumer countries. The basic philosophy for such agreements is reflected in Part IV of GATT, adopted in 1966, two years after UNCTAD I.

The specific policies of international trade demanded by developing countries which have an immediate bearing on the emerging principles of international law include the granting of preferential trade opportunities. The Generalized System of Preferences operates within a global context. For example, through most favored nation clauses in treaty practice, states may agree to bind themselves to accord beneficial trade treatment on terms not less favorable than those accorded to any third state. The example of the Lome Convention and the ACP-EEC relations in this respect suggests the feasibility of implementing trade preferences on a multilateral basis. The International Law Commission in its draft proposals on MFN treaty practice advanced the concept of most favored developing nation" treatment.(26) In the petroleum industry, to give an example, MFN treatment has been claimed by developing countries and conceded by the TNCs, for purposes of upward revision of the prices of petroleum resources. Such adjustments are made periodically, reflecting changes in the contracts entered between them.

Direct Foreign Investment, Performance of Contracts in Good
Faith, the Permanent Sovereignty of States Over Their Natural
Resources, and Freedom of Action of States

The most vocal opposition to the NIEO is directed to provisions of the
Programme of Action and the Charter of Economic Rights and Duties
of States pertaining to the scope and content of the concept of
Permanent Sovereignty, as it is applied to natural resources and to
related economic activities. The issue of compensation for nationalized
foreign interests dealt with in Article 2(2) (c) of the Charter, is
probably only marginally relevant to the other claims for achieving an
equitable redistribution of global wealth. It has become, nevertheless,
one of the more visible symbols of confrontation between the capital-
exporting industrialized countries (and the TNCs which originate from
them) and the large majority of the developing nations, who have
supported the principles stated in Article 2.

The concept of Permanent Sovereignty thus articulated in Article 2
is supported by many other subtle policy recommendations in the NIEO
declaration which, although not openly challenged, characterize the
scope and meaning of the principles of international law advocated for
the future protection of direct foreign investments. For example, the
provisions concerning political and economic independence (Articles
1,4), nonintervention (Articles 2, 5, 7, and 18), and equality (Articles 10,
17, and 32) provide the context for answering such questions as whether
a country's nationalization measures are "arbitrary," in furtherance of
"public purpose," or are otherwise "reasonable." Furthermore, the train
of resolutions on this subject adopted during 1974, including earlier
General Assembly Resolutions 3171 of December 13, 1973; 3201 of the
Sixth Special Session adopted on May 1, 1974; and 3281 proclaiming the
Charter of Economic Rights, have come to be regarded by the developed industrialized states as a departure from established international
norms in three important aspects: they fail to proscribe discriminatory
foreign wealth deprivations; they fail to mention the applicability of an
international law standard; and they do not recognize obligatory
settlement by an international tribunal of disputes concerning issues of
compensation.(27) The omission of these is made conspicuous by the
fact that an earlier U.N. Declaration on Permanent Sovereignty (1962),
accepted by the industrialized and the developing states, but voted
against by all the socialist states, did contain those references.

It may be stated briefly that the issue whether a developing country,
or for that matter any state, has the right to expropriate the property
and wealth of a foreign investor (especially when such an expropriation
is admittedly of an arbitrary nature and discriminatory in effect)
pertains, it would appear, not to the economic policies of development,
but to the right of a state to apply economic coercion for attaining its
objectives. The assumption underlying these objections is that in some
instances such deprivations may result from nationalization, and therefore the NIEO provisions should cover such situations, especially the
reference to "all economic activities" in the NIEO provision on Perma-

nent Sovereignty. Sovereignty is to cover the entire range of profits made by a corporation irrespective of the justice of its transfer pricing policies. It also entails competence to invoke and apply pricing and production control measures, not as incidents of the contractual arrangement, but as "sovereign rights" related to the ownership of the resource itself.(28)

A second objection made in respect of compensation provisions in Article 2 of the charter, is that unless direct foreign investments are legally protected from unjust deprivation, the avowed objectives of the NIEO cannot be realized. Although the NIEO charter advocates equality of treatment and a national standard, and emphasizes the procedures of direct negotiation and other internal remedies as avenues for their settlement, industrialized states believe that appropriate compensation in conformity with established international law standards is an indispensable safeguard. On the other hand, developing countries argue that any reference to established international law standards implies the classical doctrine of "prompt, effective, and full compensation" determined in accordance with the market value as stipulated by the industrialized countries – who set that value. This argument focuses on the problems of the goals of "development," the economic conditions and capabilities of the nationalizing states, the criteria of "need," and other factors to which classical doctrines of international law are characteristically indifferent. The argument is that if the developing countries enrich themselves at the expense of direct foreign investments, Western technology, research and development, capital, access to markets, and so on, then they should compensate the foreign owners adequately and appropriately. Failure to do so, it is alleged, would result in "unjust enrichment" proscribed by international law. On the key notions of what is unjust and how much is appropriate compensation, the literature embraces many experiences but abounds in controversy.(29)

As a matter of fact, much of this controversy is quite unnecessary. The practice of states, before and since the adoption of the NIEO Charter, confirms the preference of a far higher degree of conformity to the legal requirements of justice and appropriate compensation than is sometimes alleged in academic writings. The experts on this subject, especially in Western industrialized countries, readily admit that there is no basis, either in theory or in practice, to the claim that existing international law has established any norms which require that nationalizations should be for a "public purpose" or "nondiscriminatory," as between the national and foreign enterprises. The claim that there exists a customary international law norm of a static content, or an "international standard," is challenged by Latin American conceptions of international law and by current international practice.(30)

When we get into specifics, the responses to nationalization require a complex and subtle examination of the factors involved.(31) The fact that in most post-nationalization arrangements the same foreign enterprises continue in a contractual or consultancy arrangement may serve to allay claims of unjust enrichment. This may be due to the fact that, as Phillipe de Seynes mentioned, "non-renewable resources acquire value largely through international markets and those resources can be exploited only through most complex technological and logistic operations."(32) Thus there is a vicious circle in which developing countries are caught. Unless international equity is translated into practice, there will be no substitute for "national procedures."

Several "confidence building" techniques may be explored in order to secure the cooperation of Western industrialized economies for achieving rapid progress in the realization of the NIEO objectives in this area. A global economic development insurance scheme will perhaps serve to redistribute any losses that may occur. Indeed, the few instances of public debt relief forthcoming from a small number of OECD countries (and expected to be the norm in the future concerning needy cases) should influence the perceptions of private financing agencies on the need to cooperate in achieving NIEO objectives. In that process the notion of foreign investment, private as well as public, would receive a new orientation that may prove to be less inimical than is presently apprehended. Once this process is set in motion (and it has already commenced), new forms of contractual obligations will emerge. International law for development cooperation should accord them support and legitimacy.

Industrialization and Redeployment

Although the Programme of Action on the NIEO includes some general concepts of industrialization and redeployment, it is the recommendation made during the second UNIDO conference in Lima that gave concrete expression to them. The proposal that "the developed countries should encourage investors to finance industrial production projects, particularly export-oriented production, in developing countries, in agreement with the latter and within the context of their laws and regulations," has implications for transnational corporations insofar as the terms governing the transfer of capital, technology, and international trade in manufactures are concerned. Direct foreign investment policies implementing the objectives of redeployment need to be negotiated, and the terms and conditions of such contractual obligations spelled out in sufficient detail, with the full awareness that such contracts carry with them the prospect of a complete absorption of the contractual structure into the local laws and policies of the recipient state. To give an example, the NIEO Programme of Action calls for an effort "to adapt commercial practices governing transfer of technology to the requirements of the developing countries and to prevent abuse of the rights of sellers."(33) Technology, patented or not, is property not in the hands of governments but in those of private corporate enterprises. Consequently any commitment in this respect remains purely an ideal unless the transnational corporations owning the technology agree to its transfer, to its appropriate adaptation to the needs of the recipient state, and to its continuous development to meet the evolving needs of the new industrial project. The appropriate framework for achieving this objective must be developed in collaboration with the TNCs, even if financial aid is forthcoming for such projects from public governmental sources in industrialized countries. Considerable effort is being made, especially under the auspices of UNCTAD, to develop a code of conduct for the transfer of technology. But even if we assume that such a code will have a mandatory character, its acceptance at the governmental level may not be sufficient to interpret the scope of the obligations contracted by a developing country government with a transnational corporation.

Finally, the whole notion of trade liberalization is intimately connected with the developing countries' claims to the elimination of tariff and non-tariff measures in industrialized countries. The developing countries seek "redeployment" of some labor-intensive, low-technology industries from the industrialized states into their own countries. While agreement may be reached in some sectors of industry on this subject, the TNCs regard the claim as indistinguishable from any other restraining practice. A global industrialization policy, as UNIDO has pointed out, must come to terms sooner or later with the need for redeployment, not only because the poorer countries need it for a start, but also because the affluent nations will benefit from it in the long run.

Consider, for example, the developing country exports, such as textiles and leather goods, which are unlikely to have serious negative effects on overall employment in the developed countries. As Robert McNamara pointed out, the developing countries' exports of manufactured goods constitute less than 2 percent of the manufactured goods consumed by the developed nations. These very same industries are the ones heavily subsidized today in the industrialized countries to compete with exports. By abandoning excessive protectionism, the number of workers likely to be displaced will only be a tiny fraction of those displaced by shifts in technology and demand in the industrialized countries themselves. As McNamara said further, "the protectionist view overlooked the fact that the loss of jobs due to imports from the developing countries was outweighed by the increase in jobs due to the growing volume of exports to those countries made possible by the foreign exchange the developing countries are thereby able to raise."(34)

Similarly, cooperative efforts involving redeployment of industries are sought in order to shift production from some industrialized countries facing congestion and unacceptable levels of pollution, to developing countries whose industrialization efforts would benefit. The objection that such a policy will leave the developed consumer countries with mere "service industries" appears shortsighted. Clearly, in these matters intergovernmental cooperation alone cannot yield mutually beneficial results unless private banking institutions, multinational marketing agencies, and technology-supplying TNCs see that these policies are also to their own advantage. The developing countries in turn must make sustained efforts to infuse confidence and offer reliable guarantees necessary to attract major foreign investments.

Technology Transfer

The transfer of technology is essentially a process in which scientific, economic, and managerial skills are transmitted for application in the production of goods and services. The transfer of skill involves more than transhipping hardware to erect a new production center. It calls for training and requires the movement of knowhow, patent information, and new research and development inputs through selection, acquisition, and appropriate adaptation to particular contexts. Such a transfer may occur vertically from invention through adaptation to diffusion, or horizontally from one economic sector to another either within the same country or between different countries.

The strategies of technology acquisition, whether through foreign investment or by going after unpackaged technology, are intimately dependent upon the type of developmental contract designed for a given situation. In the case of a number of products, the monopoly of TNCs and their ability to control the market have imposed severe restrictions on the ability of the developing countries to obtain up-to-date improvements on a continuous basis. The NIEO objectives in this regard cannot be successfully realized unless strong institutional measures are adopted at regional and international levels to facilitate technology transfer under conditions conducive to the developmental needs of the developing countries.

The overall NIEO objectives in this area find formal enunciation in several specific contexts. For example, Article 13 of the Charter of Economic Rights and Duties of States declares the obligation to transfer technology in the following manner:

Every State has the right to benefit from the advances and developments in science and technology for the acceleration of its economic and social development.

All States should promote. . .transfer of technology, with proper regard for all legitimate interests including, inter alia, the rights and duties of holders, suppliers and recipients of technology. In particular, all States should facilitate the access of developing countries to the achievements of modern science and technology, the transfer of technology and the creation of indigenous technology for the benefit of the developing countries in forms and in accordance with procedures which are suited to their economies and their needs.

Further developments in this area have reached the point where the international community has begun to articulate the concept of technology availability as if the resource in question were part of the common heritage of mankind. Especially the proposals concerning the exploitation of seabed resources in the international area, contained in the Informal Composite Negotiating Text, envisage a legal obligation on the part of the owners of technology-holding concessions to exploit such resources and transfer the technology they devise and utilize to the proposed seabed authority under appropriate safeguards. One such safeguard is the provision to refer any disputes arising in respect of the transfer of technology to compulsory procedures of third-party settlement — something that is absent from the Charter of Economic Rights and Duties of States. But it is not so much the absence of any compulsory dispute settlement procedures as such that is likely to create difficulties, but the effect of the general technology transfer policies advocated by a large majority of United Nations member states (and endorsed in principle by the industrialized states) on their respective bargaining positions, either at the time of contract negotiation or at the time of the termination of a contract for purposes of computing the "appropriate" amount of compensation.

There are several other proposals in the NIEO declarations which carry considerable weight in discussions and negotiations concerning the transfer of technology. These include the establishment of an industrial technological information bank; the relationship between public grants made in support of research and development projects and its bearing on the right of other states to impose countervailing tariffs and other duties on products marketed utilizing such subsidized technology; the need to revise national patent systems and international conventions on patents and trademarks to meet the special needs of the developing countries; and the obligations of the developed countries to give free and full access to technologies whose transfer is not subject to private decision.

The acceptance of the seabed scheme, insofar as it relates to technology transfer, can offer useful insights for developing appropriate international mechanisms to overcome many of the commonly known impediments to the free flow of advanced technology to developing countries. The adequate protection of trade secrets, and the desire for appropriate returns for proprietary interests in patents and technology, do not stand as impediments, nor are they factors that cannot be regulated by international law. Given the necessary goodwill and a spirit of cooperation for promoting global economic development, the inherent interrelationship between technology availability and technology demand can help create new institutions and new structures for its management.(35)

An integrated approach toward this end would require coordinated efforts on the part of UNCTAD, UNIDO, and WIPO. The purpose should be to integrate technology transfer obligations into the overall structure of obligations to promote the industrial development of the developing countries. The presently formulated principles and objectives of the NIEO should be accorded concrete expression. For this purpose the agencies engaged in advising contract negotiations should explore new types of contract linkages that would ensure a continuous supply of available and appropriate technologies. Such linkages must alo, if they are to be realistic, include an appropriate role for international agencies to ensure the needed protection to technology holders under adverse conditions.

Creeping Nationalization, Outright Expropriation, and the
Obligation to Comply with the International Standard

The policies controlling intergovernmental contractual obligations, especially in matters concerning public debt, have, since the time of the
"Drago doctrine," evolved to the point that "rescheduling" (giving rise in
exceptional cases to a total write-off) is seen to have implications for
the traditional international legal principles of the recognition and
state-succession of new governments. With respect to contractual
obligations arising from agreements with transnational commercial
enterprises, the relevant legal principles are under attack in the NIEO
debates. Although under the doctrines of diplomatic protection the
distinction between public and private debts became irrelevant for all
practical purposes, arguments in favor of a "new international standard"
for judging the behavior of the deprivors of foreign wealth came
recently to be more explicitly articulated. The right to set a new
standard, admittedly of unspecified content, is claimed by the developing countries in the name of the "permanent sovereignty of states
over natural resources." In its application, the alleged doctrine is
viewed by its critics as a challenge to the basic tenets of the rule of
law governing transnational intercourse, such as pact sunt servanda,
good faith, justice, and equity.

Postwar developments in this area are characterized by a remark-
able rise in nationalizations where the newly independent nations –
including older nations that have departed from their former political
systems – began taking control of foreign enterprises as part of their
economic and social development strategy. Such take-over affected
directly the business of transnational corporations. In most cases,
because the parties involved were unable to negotiate the changes, the
existing concessionary contracts were terminated. The appropriateness
of the terms and amounts of compensation paid in such instances was a
matter of bitter controversy. Despite the accumulation of a rich and
varied state practice, the formal enunciation of the legal principles and
policies relevant for their interpretation and application has remained
vague and ambivalent. Indeed, in a recent Arbitral Award between
Texaco Overseas Petroleum Company/California Asiatic Oil Company
and the Government of The Libyan Arab Republic, it was stated that:

> The fact that various nationalization measures in disregard of
> previously concluded agreements have been accepted in fact by
> those who were affected, either private companies or by the
> states of which they were nationals, cananot be interpreted as
> recognition by international practice of such a rule; the amicable
> settlements which have taken place having been inspired basical-
> ly by considerations of expediency and not of legality. . . .(36)

The specific NIEO principles cited in support of developing countries' arguments are contained in Article 2 of the Charter of Economic
Rights and Duties of States. As mentioned earlier, there are three basic

objections raised by the industrialized states to the provisions of Article 2.

First, there is no mention in Article 2 that contractual commitments entered into in good faith are binding. If a contract contains a so-called "freezing clause" under which the contracting state agrees not to invoke any of its future legislative policies to require changes in the contract, then that party, it is contended, is precluded from altering the contract. The protagonists of the doctrine of "good faith" are silent on the policies that ought to be operative when the essential contractual equality ceases to exist because of the changes in the market conditions, pricing structure, resource consumption practices, natural well-being, or other similar factors. The essential point to be observed, especially in connection with economic development contracts or concessions, is that at some point in time, probably sooner rather than later, the developing state may not only find it desirable to exercise its full control over all its economic activities, but is expected to do so.

The essential difficulty in this dilemma is not so much the applicability of the doctrine of "good faith," which is also mentioned in the NIEO Charter, but the objectives for which it can be invoked. When the claim for renegotiation is found unacceptable it often meets with the claim of pacta sunt servanda.

As Dr. Asante pointed out, renegotiation is generally rejected as a helpful tool for maintaining contractual obligations.(37) On the other hand, the reason for enforcing a contract, especially a long-term concessionary contract, is precisely to protect those interests which the corporations seek to ensure through the operation of law, outside the legislation of the host state.(38)

The NIEO Charter does not recognize that in the event of a nationalization or similar measure affecting the proprietary interests of a foreign corporation, the doctrine of a minimum international standard, not the domestic national policies of the expropriating state, should be applicable. The argument whether the compensation payable is to be in accordance with classical international law, namely "prompt, full, and effective payment," or whether it is to be "appropriate compensation" as understood by member states in 1962 when they adopted the Declaration on Permanent Sovereignty, cannot be fully answered without taking into account both the nature of the contractual arrangement involved, and the political and economic features of the international market concerning the particular resource affected.(39) Consequently, in the context of evolving international economic relationships, there is no presumption of an international standard of a static content, nor any question that the actions of the developing countries must be judged in terms of a minimum international standard essential to safeguard the interests of both the capital-exporting and the developing countries.

Discussions on the subject of restrictive business practices in UNCTAD and in the intergovernmental United Nations Commission on Transnational Corporations, touched on the magnitude and complexity of the issues requiring international regulation. On the one hand, the developing countries are dependent upon the capital, the technology, and the market information supplied by transnational corporations. On the other hand, their own experience has been that many of the largest transnational enterprises operating in their territory control the buying and selling policies of their local subsidiaries. Investment-related decisions, including access to the capital of private banking institutions; the organization and location of a subsidiary; what it should manufacture; to whom it should or should not sell; from where the technology and raw materials may be purchased and at what prices; and, if it concerns extractive industries, the qualitative and quantitative decisions related to the resources exploited, are all matters that cannot be captured fully by proposals restricted to controlling competition. These are obviously matters that affect international trade, and the future prospects of economic development in developing countries. Obviously, if the developing countries want to attract direct foreign investment and advanced technology, they must offer the investors incentives to enter into agreements. The developing countries, fully conscious of their own interests, are ready to subscribe to standards of international law (witness the recent Japan-Egypt foreign investment Agreement(40)) which can also ensure adequate protection of the basic interests of the industrialized countries. Fair treatment, economic stability, and an opportunity to realize a fair return on capital invested are the minimum requirements for promoting international cooperation.

The critical question is whether, in the context of the NIEO, the objectives of both sides can be achieved. The Andean Code on direct foreign investment, formulated by the countries of Latin America, is one attempt. The success or failure of such attempts will in large measure depend on how transnational corporations will adapt themselves, both to remain in business, and to be a vehicle for the realization of the aspirations of the vast majority of the world's sovereign nations.

As already indicated, the NIEO proposals on TNCs cover a number of other matters, such as their political influence in the formation of the foreign policies of the host as well as of the home countries, intervention in the internal affairs of the host countries, the obligation to respect the laws and the economic and social objectives of the host countries, and so on. These propositions are least controversial when discussed as desirable objectives in international fora, but it is far from clear how they are to be related to specific actions of states, including measures of nationalization or breaches of the good faith observance of contractual commitments. The adoption of a comprehensive code of conduct to regulate the activities of transnational corporations may in fact serve to promote the ideals of competition cherished by the free market system because, to the extent that such ideals reflect the needs of global economic development, they will also be applicable to the corporations established by developing countries, which are generally not private enterprises but state owned trading companies.

The specific decisions of international judicial and arbitral bodies in the nationalization and expropriation controversies fall short of clarifying policies for the determination of what is an "appropriate compensation." This is in part attributable to the "mystifying secrecy" that exists on the financial position of the TNCs and the inability of states to obtain full disclosure. There is need for appropriate standards of accounting and reporting of corporate activities, subject to proper safeguards to protect the legitimate areas of confidentiality.

Given the enormous potential of TNCs as agents for development and modernization, it is a pity that their legal structure has not been developed to face the tasks awaiting them. As William Halal has pointed out, in the current post-industrial era of Western developed society, the global corporation must shed its veil and come into the open to play a responsible role.(41)

Thirdly, it has been pointed out that even if classical notions of international law and international standards cannot blindly be applied to changing economic and political relations among states, the empirical content of the existing standard cannot be left to the unilateral decision of one side, certainly not to the claimant itself. Therefore, it has been urged that the NIEO Charter, if it is to serve as a basis for the further development of international economic law, must provide for binding third-party settlement of disputes. Indeed, in the matter of transfer of technology and seabed mining, future international agreement on the principles concerning the Law of the Sea advocated by the developing countries is critically dependent upon such a dispute settlement procedure. The NIEO should be no different. In most instances of nationalization, the parties concerned utilize the negotiating framework for bargaining the precise content of the compensation payable. This may not be the best procedure for making objective determinations as to what is appropriate and equitable in a situation. But since direct foreign investment is a function of the trustworthiness of the developing country seeking resources, and of the profitability of the venture, the basic minimum standard demanded by international law must cover the financial risk as well as the profits accrued by the transaction. The difficulty lies in projecting viable policies for determining what constitutes "appropriate" compensation and profit.

The developing countries themselves are ambivalent on these questions. Having established the principles that nationalization is an act of sovereignty and as such not contrary to international law, and that the state whose natural resources are involved in the exploitation and marketing has full permanent sovereignty irrespective of the jurisdiction involved, it is now desirable to clarify comprehensively and in sufficient detail the policies governing direct foreign investment. As Joseph Sanford correctly pointed out, such an effort is likely to influence future state practice and provide the proper basis for international law in the new international economic order.(42)

THE TASK AHEAD

The foregoing discussion has focused on the major objections to the substantive NIEO proposals made by the developing countries for a new international economic order, and has considered the role of international law in responding to the proposals. As regards the renegotiation of public debts, it is essential to clarify the scope and content of the general policies governing transfers in real resources. Such policies should also address the impact of currency fluctuations and changing trade preferences of the industrialized countries on the economies of developing countries. Serious consideration should be given to an international monetary fund based fully on SDRs, with regulatory powers to periodically adjust the values of SDRs to meet the development needs of Third World countries. In the area of private resource transfers, the Charter of Economic Rights and Duties of States should be followed by a comprehensive declaration of principles clarifying the general policies pertaining to direct foreign investment. The policies in question should include the fundamental principles governing investment and development.

The criteria governing foreign investment acceptable to developing countries, and the principles relating to the protection of, and appropriate return from, investments which capital-exporting nations consider essential, are not, and need not be, mutually incompatible. Many developing countries have declared in their domestic legislations the detailed policy considerations pertaining to direct foreign investment by private transnational corporations. As a first step, the General Assembly should undertake a survey of the most commonly accepted principles. Based upon such a survey and on the practice of many important developing countries, a United Nations convention on direct foreign investment and economic development should be proposed. It is not enough to formulate generalizations which are least controversial, or declare objectives as if they would determine or control future behavior. What is needed is a careful specification of the policies, the formulation of the precise content of the legal obligations they entail, and the specification of the situations to which they apply. Since it is simply not possible to envisage all the myriad contingencies likely to emerge to which such policies may be relevant, it is desirable to envisage a mutually acceptable system of objective and dependable third-party settlement procedures. There is no reason why, within such a system of compulsory settlement of disputes, third-party decision makers should not be required to apply the principles of that convention as a basis for resolving particular disputes. Given a sufficient realization of the interdependencies affecting the economic interests of the developed and the developing countries, the criteria to be recommended for the interpretation and application of contractual commitments can be made explicit. If transnational corporations shy away from demands to engage in periodic renegotiations of concession or investment agreements, the developing countries can invoke the protection of such a convention in support of their goals.

International capital movement is only one (no doubt important) leg of the tripod on which a NIEO must rest. The other two bases, namely technology transfer and access to markets, should also be seen as interrelated goals. International financial organizations should evolve appropriate procedures designed to promote the economic well-being of developing countries without necessarily requiring that their production facilities be geared to export markets.

The social and political consequences of economic development programs tied to export markets has not yet been fully comprehended. In the matter of direct foreign investment arrangements involving private banks, the IMF should serve as a trustee to guarantee an appropriate return on such investments, by drawing from possible surpluses in trade of both developed and developing countries. If the proposed convention adequately elaborates the principles of international law governing foreign investment, it will serve to encourage transnational corporations to undertake technology transfers, redeployment of industries, and new resource investments within developing countries with full knowledge of the fundamental legal principles of the international economic order which support them. For the developing countries the new order affords opportunities to bring to bear their new capabilities in the areas of shipping, insurance, transportation, and marketing of their products. The impact on their interests of fluctuations in commodity prices, and of changing patterns of trade, may then be appropriately reflected to justify their demands for revision of their existing contractual or concessionary arrangements with transnationals. In short, international law will be enriched to serve the important functions of the integration and regulation of global economic transactions.

NOTES

(1) Although the demands for a NIEO are termed as "the ultimatums of the rebellious poor countries" it is also claimed ". . .the notion that conscious human action can change the 'order' of things, even human things, and that mankind can attack world poverty in a systematic way with ultimate success is a fundamentally Western idea. . ." Richard N. Cooper, "A New International Economic Order for Mutual Gain," Foreign Policy 26 (Spring 1977).

(2) These efforts have been recalled by scholars even before the formal NIEO declarations. See Wolfgang Friedmann, "Corporate Power, Government by Private Groups and the Law," 57 Columbia L.R. 155 (1957) and "The Relevance of International Law to the Processes of Economic and Social Development," in Falk and Black, eds., The Future of the International Legal Order, Vol. II, pp. 3-36 (1970).

(3) Ernst U. Petersmann, "The New International Economic Order — Principles, Politics and International Law," in Macdonald, Morris, and Johnston, eds., The International Law and Policy of Human Welfare, pp. 449-471 (1978).

(4) Samual Asante has pointed out that these legal concepts served as "the fundamental underpinnings of the old economic order" and operate as impediments for achieving global economic justice and equity.

> The system which has been the object of much rhetoric at the United Nations and other political fora is supported by a formidable and highly sophisticated armoury of legal and commercial concepts which need a radical revision if the international economic order is to be effectively restructured. . . .First, concepts such as ownership, contract, corporate personality which appear quite innocuous within the context of a municipal legal system may have grave implications when transplanted into the sphere of transnational transactions. Second, it is an established legal tradition in Europe and, to some extent, America, to refer to these legal concepts as the colourless tools of a legal system. Yet any perceptive observer will concede that these concepts connote discrete value systems of a distinct individualistic bias, which are often manifestly inimical to the aspirations and development goals of new nations. They should therefore not be accorded the status of immutable and universal postulates.

(5) Development Forum 6, no. 9 (October 1978).

(6) Echoing this sentiment, the U.S. Under-Secretary of State for Economic Affairs, Richard N. Cooper, wrote:

> The calls for a new international order raise a host of questions, some concerning the philosophical foundations of claims for resource transfers between nations — or indeed between individuals — some concerning the system of governance at the global level, and some concerning the desirability and the feasibility of the particular proposals that have been advanced. These questions themselves represent a response, often critical or sceptical, about the nature of the claims and the character of the proposals put forward. . . .Human "solidarity" is not a sentiment in harmony with zero-sum thinking. If we want to achieve global solidarity rather than global discord, the emphasis must be shifted to the areas in which there are possibilities for mutual gain. . . .Such a shift in focus would substantially improve the prospects for a new international economic order.

(7) See Clive Schmithoff, The Sources of the Law of International Trade 70 (1964).

(8) For an excellent survey of the basic concerns of the global order system from this perspective see Ronald Macdonald, Gerald Morris, and Douglas Johnston, "The International Law of Human Welfare — Concept, Experience and Priorities," in op. cit., 3, 3-81; Jenks, The Common Law

of Mankind 17 (1958); and Richard Falk, "Historical Tendencies, Modernizing and Revolutionary Nations and the International Legal Order," Howard L.J. 8 (1962): 128-151.

(9) OECD Declaration on International Investment and Multinational Enterprises, reproduced in Int'l. Leg. Mat. 15 (1976); UNCTAD: Revised Report of the Groups of Experts on Transfer of Technology TD/AC.1/11 (1977) reprinted in Int'l. Leg. Mat. 17 (1978). See also Sanjaga Lall: Developing Countries and Multinational Corporations, Commonwealth Economic Paper, No. 5 (London, 1976).

(10) There have been limited, albeit indirect participatory opportunities afforded to NGOs and Corporations in the deliberations of the U.N. Commission on Transnational Corporations and in the 3rd U.N. Conference on the Law of the Sea. The constitutive processes for policy clarification, in their formal setting, still suffer from procedural infirmities which prevent such non-state entities, crucial actors in the value processes under consideration, from playing a responsible role.

(11) See Brower and Tepe, "Charter of Economic Rights and Duties of States – A Reflection or Rejection of International Law?" International Lawyer 9 (1975); G. White, "A New International Economic Order," I.C.L.Q. 24 (1975); Petersmann, op. cit., note 3. Compare: A.O. Adede, "International Law and Property of Aliens – The Old Order Changeth," Malaya L.R. 19 (1977), 175-193; and M. Sornarajah, "Compensation for Expropriation: The Emergence of New Standards," J. World Trade Law 13 (1979): 108-131.

(12) See Sanford, op. cit., 11.

(13) See for example L. Henken, "Arctic Anti-Pollution: Does Canada Make or Break International Law?" A.J.I.L. 65 (1971): 131.

(14) See Richard Falk's comments in "Diverging Anglo-American Attitudes to International Law," Ga. J. Int'l. and Comp. L. 2 (1972): 29.

(15) "Award on the merits in dispute between Texaco Overseas Petroleum Company/California Asiatic Oil Co., and the Government of the Libyan Arab Republic," transl. in International Legal Materials 18 (1978): 1-37.

(16) See McDougal, Lasswell and Chen, "The Protection of Aliens from Discrimination and World Public Order: Responsibility of States conjoined with Human Rights," A.J.I.L. 70 (1976): 432.

(17) See The Objectives of the New International Economic Order, for a classification of the basic 25 or 30 issues involved in the current debates.

(18) See Joseph Gold, "Financial Assistance by the International Monetary Fund – Law and Practice," IMF Pamphlet 27 (Washington, 1979); Stephen Silard, "The Impact of the International Monetary Fund on International Trade," Journal of World Trade Law 2 (1968): 121. J.J. Polak: "Thoughts on an International Monetary Fund based fully on the SDR," I.M.F. Pamphlet 28 (1979).

(19) See Patricia W. Fagen, "The Links between Human Rights and Basic Needs," Report of the Centre for International Policy, "Background," Spring 1978, Washington, D.C.

(20) Ibid., p. 11.

(21) From a legal point of view, the impressive aid record of Arab Oil exporting countries has two important implications. The first is that the conduct of these states contributes to the evolution of new legal rules in the sphere of international economic cooperation. For even though contemporary international law does not create a legal obligation upon richer states to provide assistance to the less fortunate countries, a moral obligation to this effect is gradually hardening into a binding international custom. Present aid efforts of Arab oil producing states are accelerating the establishment of this custom. . . .Elements of the opinio juris, necessary in the conventional theory for completing the custom-making process, may thus be discerned in the oil producers' behaviour even at this stage. . . .on account of recent Arab practices. . .customary international law has already established an obligation of aid giving in favour of poorer countries.

Ibraham Shihata, "Arab Oil Policies and the New International Economic Order," Virginia J.I.L. 16 (1976): 278-279.

(22) Oscar Schachter pointed out,

This is the central feature of the contemporary international law of development. When we reflect on it, it may seem extraordinary how we have come to accept it and how far reaching its implications may extend. Can we reconcile need as a basis of entitlement with other fundamental legal principles such as equality among states or their established rights? How can need fit into the still prevailing conception of a world market economy based on principles of comparative advantage and non-discriminatory trade?

(See Oscar Schachter, "The Evolving International Law of Development," Columbia J. Trans. L. 15 (1976): 1-16.)

(23) See for example, M. Sornarajah, "Compensation for Expropriation – The Emergence of New Standards," Journal of World Trade Law 13 (1979): 108-131.

(24) See A.O. Adede, "Loan Agreements between Developing Countries and Foreign Commercial Banks – Reflections on some Legal and Economic Issues," Syracuse Journal of International Law and Commerce 5 (1978): 235-268.

(25) See for example, Oscar Schachter, "Just Prices in World Markets: Proposals de lege ferenda," A.J.I.L. 69 (1975): 101.

(26) See U.N. Doc. A/CN. 4/309, April 11, 1978; Report of the International Law Commission," July 1978, G.A.O.R., 33rd Session, pp. 6-178 (Article 21).

(27) See Generally Burns H. Weston, "Constructive Takings under International Law – A Modest Foray into the Problem of Creeping Expropriations," Virginia J.I.L. 16 (1975): 103.

(28) For example, Dr. Shihata wrote: "Nothing in the present system of international law prevents a producing country from selling its primary products at whatever prices it chooses to fix. Indeed the right of every country to freely dispose of its natural wealth is an integral part of the universally acknowledged principle that a state possesses sovereignty over all of its natural resources." Shihata: "Arab Oil Policies and the New International Economic Order."

(29) See, for example, the Reports of the Secretary General on the subject of Permanent Sovereignty of States over Natural Resources, especially Doc. A/9716 of September 1974 and ECOSOC Doc. E/5986 of May 1977.

(30) Note Sornarajah, "Compensation for Expropriation"; Andrew N. Onejeme: "The Law of Natural Resources Development: Agreements Between Developing Countries and Foreign Investors," Syr. J. Int'l and Comm. 5 (1977): 1-52. They analyze the impact of the various General Assembly Resolutions on the content of the legal norms applicable for the interpretation and application of concession agreements.

(31) Oscar Schachter points out the dynamics of compensation negotiations, which appear to answer in part the objections leveled at the NIEO declaration mentioned earlier:

> When a controversy arises over expropriation, it is almost certain that issues of fair treatment and "appropriate" compensation will be raised within the negotiating or settlement framework established by the expropriating government. The argument then is not on the issue of national competence but

about the specific circumstances and the criteria to be applied. We can reasonably assume that the perception of these issues will be substantially affected by standards developed in other contexts, whether they are stated explicitly or not. This would be so even though the references to governing law are limited to the legislation of the expropriating country. (Schachter, Sharing the World's Resources, (1977), pp. 53-55.)

(32) Philippe de Seynes, "Transnational Corporations and Development," C.T.C. Reporter 1 (1976).

(33) UNIDO, Lima Declaration and Plan of Action on Industrial Development and Cooperation, ID/CONF. 3/31, March 26, 1975.

(34) Robert McNamara's Statement to the Joint Annual Meetings of the World Bank and IMF, as reported in Development Forum 6, no. 9 (1978).

(35) See David Silverstein, "Property Protection for Deep-Sea Mining Technology in return for Technology Transfer: New Approach to Seabed Controversy," Fletcher Forum 1 (1978): 15-41; Rene-Jean Dupuy, "The Implications for the Developing Countries of the Composite Negotiating Texts Provisions on Marine Technology Transfer," Pacem in Maribus 8 (Mexico, 1977).

(36) See the Libyan Arbitration Award, op. cit. It is worth recalling here that at the time of the debates on the adoption of the Charter of Economic Rights and Duties of States, the delegate of Canada, speaking on the proposal of an additional third paragraph to the present Article 2 requiring states to fulfill in good faith their international obligations, had this to say: "The third paragraph proposed for Article 2. . . prejudged neither the content of international law relating to foreign investment, nor the sources of such law. It merely sought to establish the principle that, in this important area of international relations, the rule of law is to apply among states. . . ." ("Current Issues of International Law of Particular Importance to Canada," Department of External Affairs, October 1976, pp. 38-41).

(37) Renegotiation is now an incontrovertible fact of the current investment process throughout the developing world. . . yet investors are loathe to accept express stipulations for renegotiation in investment agreements. Why? Investors are understandably concerned about the security of their deal and this yearning for certainty induces them to maintain the pretence that a deal once concluded would endure. . . . Multi-national corporations protest that renegotiation is fundamentally offensive to the financing arrangements made with their financiers which are predicated on the assumption that the undertaking will yield a certain return at a specific time to amortize the investment. Some investors concede that they would be prepared to honour an invitation to

renegotiate but they argue that it is a bad precedent to expressly provide for it. (Asante, op. cit.)

(38) The emphasis on the contractual nature of the legal relation between the investor is intended to bring about an equilibrium between the goal of the general interest sought by such relation and the profitability which is necessary for the pursuit of the task entrusted to the private enterprise. The effect is also to ensure to the private contracting party a certain stability which is justified by the considerable investments which it makes in the country concerned. The investor must in particular be protected against legislative uncertainties, that is to say the risks of the municipal law of the host country being modified, or against any government measures which would lead to an abrogation of rescission of the contract. Hence the insertion of the so-called stabilization clauses: These clauses tend to remove all or part of the agreement from the internal law and to provide for its correlative submission to sui generis rules. . . or to a system which is properly an international law system. . . . (The Libyan Arbitration Award, op. cit.)

(39) As Wilfred Jenks wrote:

The test is the 'ordinary standards of civilisation'; the common denominator is the 'practice of civilised nations'; the criterion is the judgement of a 'reasonable and impartial man.' These are all conceptions so general that their content will necessarily be determined by the policy of the times. The diplomatic protection of citizens abroad has often been associated in the past with the exercise of military, political or economic pressure by stronger against weaker States and it is therefore not a matter for surprise that a growing resistance to the concept of an international standard should have been an almost inevitable feature of a period of sharp criticism of neo-colonialism; but an international standard, fairly applied, is both so fundamental an element in the concept of internationally guaranteed basic human rights and so essential a prerequisite of any mutually beneficial international economic intercourse that the concept may be expected to reassert itself in deference to overriding considerations of international public policy which are entitled to claim, and may be expected to receive, general acceptance. (C.W. Jenks, The Prospects of International Adjudication, (1964), pp. 514-515). (The footnotes in the original are omitted.)

(40) See Egypt-Japan: "Agreement on the Encouragement and Reciprocal Protection of Investment," Int'l. Leg. Mat. 18 (1979): 44.

(41) William Halal, in Meadows and McCollom, eds., Alternatives to Growth, vol. II (1978).

(42)The need for investment capital will remain, however, and
even if significantly diminished will continue to be, potentially
at least, a major tool at the disposal of development planners in
the developing countries. The extent to which this tool is used
will depend largely upon whether the commercial motives of the
investors are perceived, by either side, as inconsistent with the
sovereignty and development objectives of the host country.
There is no inherent reason why these two objectives should be
inconsistent.   It is for the investors and the development
planners to devise investment arrangements which respond to
both objectives. If they are successful, bilateral state practice
will generate a new body of customary international law respect-
ing both the sovereignty of the host state and the legitimate
interests of the investor. (Joseph Sanford, op. cit., 11, p. 493.)

Index

113

Temperate Zone Nations, 4
Third World Development, 7
Tokyo Round. <u>See</u> General Agree-
    ment on Tariffs and Trade
    (GATT)
Transnational Corporations, 19,
    22, 26, 32, 34, 35, 49,
    52-54, 79, 80-81, 83-85,
    97, 98, 102
  Co-ownership, 54
  International Code of conduct
    for, 83
  Restrictive Business Practices,
    83, 92
  Subcontracting, 48-49
  <u>See also</u> Foreign Direct
        Investment, United
        Nations Commission
        on Transnational
        Corporations

Unemployment, 4, 7, 25, 29
  Charter, 76
  International Law Commission,
    90, 95-96, 97-98
  Second Development Decade,
    94, 95
  United Nations Commission
        on Transnational Cor-
        porations, 83, 84
  United Nations Conference
        on the Law of the Sea,
        49, 92
  United Nations Conference on
        Trade and Development
        (UNCTAD), 28, 39, 48,
        49, 50, 84, 99
    Code of Conduct for
        Maritime Confer-
        ences, 49
    Trade and Development
        Board, 96
  United Nations Industrial
        Development Organiza-
        tion (UNIDO) Confer-
        ence, Lima, 99
  United Nations System, 56, 57
  World Intellectual Property
        Organization (WIPO),
        99

Unemployment (cont.)
  <u>See also</u> International Civil
        Service
United States, 12, 18, 19, 21-22,
    29, 38
  Dollar, 5, 13, 19, 21, 23, 24,
    49
  Imports, 20
  Treasury Bills, 12

Vietnam, 23, 27, 29

Welfare, 89
World Bank, 49, 58
  International Bank for Re-
        construction and
        Development (IBRD),
        90
  International Finance Cor-
        poration (IFC), 90
  <u>See also</u> Aid
World War I, 5
World War II, 5

Zero-sum, 79-80

About the Editors
and Contributors

ERVIN LASZLO – Director, UNITAR/CEESTEM Project on the New International Economic Order.

JOEL KURTZMAN – Coordinator, Project to Create a New International Economic Order, UNITAR.

ALDO FERRER – Director of the Centro de Coyuntura (Instituto de Desarrollo Economico y Social) Buenos Aires.

JORGE FONTANALS – Centro de Estudios del Desarrollo (CENDES) Universidad Central de Venezuela, Caracas.

MICHAEL HUDSON – Economic Consultant, New York.

ENRIQUE OTEIZA – Director of CRESAL-UNESCO (Centro Regional Para la Education Superior en America Latina y el Caribe), Caracas.

FERNANDO PORTA – Centro de Estudios del Desarrollo (CENDES) Universidad Central de Venezuela, Caracas.

K. VENKATA RAMAN – Queens University, Kingston.

SUSANA SCHKOLNIK – CRESAL-UNESCO, Caracas.

VLADISLAV B. TIKHOMIROV – UNITAR, New York.

MIGUEL S. WIONCZEK – El Colegio de Mexico, Mexico City.